In bite-size pieces, Zach invite
lowers of Jesus and to find that
others but in the opinion and fear or the One who loves us and gave
his life for us. Zach pushes us to look at our motives and concerns
and to ask why we feel or believe the things about ourselves that we
do. When those things are wrong and are rooted in the fear of others, we are either believing something about God that is not true or
not believing something about God that we need to. I look forward
to recommending this devotional to the folks in our church.

   —**Jackson Crum**, Lead Pastor, Park Community Church,
   Chicago

Zach Schlegel is one of my favorite people and pastors. I've known
him for over a decade and have had the joy of serving with him
for years. Meet him, and what will strike you is his strength—
his grip, his physical thickness, and how unbelievably deep his
voice is! But once you get to know him, what will strike you is his
weakness—which you will know only because, in his humility,
he lets you know. If you fear others, this book can serve as a GPS
that God will use to get you out of that person-fearing country,
with Zach as a wonderful guide. I've read every word, and it all
sounds like Zach—a man who seems to know the Bible as well as
he knows his own heart. Profit your soul with this book.

   —**Mark Dever**, Senior Pastor, Capitol Hill Baptist Church,
   Washington, DC; President, 9Marks

Fearing other people is a dreadful, paralyzing condition. It is a
snare, a source of anguish, a root of unbelief, a killer of joy. In
Fearing Others, Zach Schlegel helps us to see the true anatomy of
this condition and the only remedy for it: the grace of God in the
gospel of Jesus Christ. These careful reflections on Scripture will
call you to a holy fear that puts all other fears to death.

   —**John Henderson**, Council Member, Biblical Counseling
   Coalition ; Executive Director, Center for Church Equipping

The fear of men is the root of frustration's fruit in our lives. Zach helps us to remember that this is a malady that needs to not only be erased but also displaced with the fear of God. And he does more than just tell us that we need to do this; he takes us by the hand and shows us how. This is insightful, careful, enjoyable, and warm counsel from a seasoned pastor. Experience the freedom that comes when we give our hearts, hopes, and fears to the only One who is strong enough to carry them.

—**John Onwuchekwa**, Lead Pastor, Cornerstone Church, Atlanta; Author, *Prayer: How Praying Together Shapes the Church.*

Pastor Zach Schlegel has done us all a great favor by writing this book about fear and how to deal with it. His insights are biblical, and his counsel is practical. I wish I had read a book like this while I was still a seminary student beginning my pastoral ministry. It would have made me much more effective in my home and in the church.

—**Warren W. Wiersbe**, Author, Be Series Bible Commentaries; Former Pastor, Moody Church, Chicago

FEARING OTHERS

31-Day Devotionals for Life

A Series

Deepak Reju
Series Editor

Addictive Habits: Changing for Good, by David R. Dunham
After an Affair: Pursuing Restoration, by Michael Scott Gembola
Anger: Calming Your Heart, by Robert D. Jones
Assurance: Resting in God's Salvation, by William P. Smith
Contentment: Seeing God's Goodness, by Megan Hill
Doubt: Trusting God's Promises, by Elyse Fitzpatrick
Fearing Others: Putting God First, by Zach Schlegel
Grief: Walking with Jesus, by Bob Kellemen
Pornography: Fighting for Purity, by Deepak Reju

FEARING OTHERS

PUTTING
GOD FIRST

ZACH SCHLEGEL

P U B L I S H I N G
P.O. BOX 817 • PHILLIPSBURG • NEW JERSEY 08865-0817

Scripture quotations are from the ESV® Bible (The Holy Bible, English Standard Version®), copyright © 2001 by Crossway, a publishing ministry of Good News Publishers. Used by permission. All rights reserved.

Italics within Scripture quotations indicate emphasis added.

Printed in the United States of America

Library of Congress Cataloging-in-Publication Data

Names: Schlegel, Zach, author.
Title: Fearing others : putting God first / Zach Schlegel.
Description: Phillipsburg : P&R Publishing, 2019. | Series: 31-day devotionals for life | Includes bibliographical references.
Identifiers: LCCN 2018043389| ISBN 9781629955001 (pbk.) | ISBN 9781629955018 (epub) | ISBN 9781629955025 (mobi)
Subjects: LCSH: Fear--Religious aspects--Christianity. | Interpersonal relations--Religious aspects--Christianity. | Devotional literature.
Classification: LCC BV4908.5 .S35 2019 | DDC 248.4--dc23
LC record available at https://lccn.loc.gov/2018043389

Contents

Tips for Reading This Devotional   7

Introduction   9

Understand and Identify Your Fear of Others

Day 1: We Obey What We Fear   15

Day 2: Monument Building   17

Day 3: Watch Out! It's a Trap!   19

Day 4: The Difficulty of Waiting   21

Day 5: Busy, Busy, Busy   23

Day 6: The Fear of Falling   25

Day 7: The Surprising Source of Confidence   27

Day 8: Confidence in Your Insufficiency   29

Day 9: The Grasshopper Syndrome   31

Day 10: Keeping People at a Distance   33

Day 11: Don't Take It Personally   35

Day 12: You Shall Not Covet   37

Overcome Your Fear of Others

Day 13: Overcome Your Fear of Others by Fearing God   41

Day 14: Fan the Flame   43

Day 15: Remember That God Is Mindful of You   45

Day 16: Relax; You're Not the Expert on You   47

Day 17: Take the Leap of Obedience   49

Day 18: Redefine True Greatness   51

Day 19: Know God's Purpose for Your Life   53

Day 20: Embrace the Accusations   55

Day 21: Fight Fear with Prayer   57

Day 22: Look to Your Future Hope   59

Day 23: Compete to Love, Not to Be Loved   61

Day 24: Know Who You Are   63

Day 25: Fight Fear with Thankfulness   65

Day 26: Rejoice—God Is for You!   67

Day 27: Learn True Contentment   69

Day 28: Face the What-Ifs of Life   71

Day 29: Walk in the Light   73

Day 30: Serve Your Father Who Sees in Secret   75

Day 31: Pray for a United Heart   77

Conclusion   79

Acknowledgments   81

Notes   83

Suggested Resources for the Fight   87

Tips for Reading This Devotional

EARLY IN OUR MARRIAGE, my wife and I lived on the top floor of a town house, in a small one-bedroom apartment. Whenever it rained, leaks in the roof would drip through the ceiling and onto our floors. I remember placing buckets in different parts of the apartment and watching the water slowly drip, one drop at a time. I put large buckets out and thought, *It'll take a while to fill them.* The water built up over time, and often I was surprised at how quickly those buckets filled up, overflowing if I didn't pay close enough attention.

This devotional is just like rain filling up a bucket. It's slow, and it builds over time. Just a few verses every day. Drip. Drip. Drip. Just a few drops of Scripture daily to satiate your parched soul.

We start with Scripture. God's Word is powerful. In fact, it's the most powerful force in the entire universe.[1] It turns the hearts of kings, brings comfort to the lowly, and gives spiritual sight to the blind. It transforms lives and turns them upside down. We know that the Bible is God's very own words, so we read and study it to know God himself.

Our study of Scripture is practical. Theology should change how we live. It's crucial to connect the Word with your struggles. Often, as you read this devotional, you'll see the word *you* because Zach speaks directly to you, the reader. The readings contain a mixture of reflection questions and practical suggestions. You'll get much more from this experience if you answer the questions and do the practical exercises. Don't skip them. Do them for the sake of your own soul.

Our study of Scripture is worshipful. Fear of your fellow man can rule your life. It leads you to worship the wrong things: other people's opinions and affirmation, and especially success in others' eyes. "What does he think?" "What if I don't fit in?" "What if I don't get this done? Will my boss be mad at me?" "What if they don't like me?" You can't let these fears rule your life.

Fundamentally, any struggle with fearing others is a worship problem. Fear of the Lord is the beginning of knowledge and wisdom (see Prov. 1:7), but sadly, it often doesn't come first. We lose ourselves in the sea of other people's opinions, and fear of others overwhelms us. I often try to survive on my own rather than depending on others. I build monuments to myself. I walk around scared of rejection from others. I fight back a sense of failure over my life or something I did. My parents or my boss or my spouse says something that rules my heart more than it should. Fearing others, and its debris, like shrapnel on a war-torn field, are spread out all over my life. The Lord calls out to us, "Fear *me*. Put *me* first. Seek first *my* kingdom. Why would you fear *others* more than *me*?" The goal of our lives is to fear God, not fear others.

If you find this devotional helpful (and I trust that you will!), reread it in different seasons of your life. Work through it this coming month, and then come back to it a year from now, to remind yourself how to overcome your fear of others.

This devotional is *not* meant to be a comprehensive guide to fighting your fear of others. Good volumes are already written for that purpose. Buy them and make good use of them. You'll see several resources listed at the end of the book.

That's enough for now. Let's begin.

Deepak Reju

Introduction

I wonder what they think of me.
Did they notice when I left? Did they care?
Do they think I'm pretty?
Do they think I'm smart?
Do they think I'm important?
What if I try this and fail?
What if I don't meet their expectations? What if I let them down?

Have you ever asked yourself a question like that? Often, such a question has a heart problem underneath it—a problem called the *fear of man*. Fear isn't *just* being frightened of someone; it can involve being desperate to gain something that we think we need (respect, attention, love, approval) or the frantic concern that we'll lose it once we have it. In that sense, what we fear controls us, drives our agenda, determines our mood, and enslaves us. Ed Welch describes fear of others happening when "we replace God with people. Instead of biblically guided fear of the Lord, we fear others."[1]

Recognizing fear of others in our lives can be difficult. Some of us have lived under its rule for so long that the fear of man has become background noise—as unnoticed as breathing. But just because we can't see it doesn't mean it's not there. I remember, during my first year of marriage, coming back early to our one-bedroom apartment in Chicago to do some housecleaning. As I disinfected the toilets and vacuumed the living room, I remember thinking, *Katie's going to love this. She's going to walk in and be overcome with gratitude. She'll probably start thinking about how lucky she is to have married a guy like me who would do stuff like this.* (You don't realize how ridiculous your thoughts are until you write them down like this).

9

But when Katie walked in the door that night, she didn't say a word. *Maybe she didn't notice the bathroom yet. I just need to give it a little time.* We started making supper, but still no comment. *Maybe she had a long day and is distracted. Or maybe she's so stunned, she doesn't know what to say. I'll give her a little more time.* When we sat down to dinner, I pulled up my chair, ready to receive her praise. But instead, all I got was, "How was your day, honey?" *How was my day? How ungrateful can she be?* It was the last straw. "How was my day?! Did you notice how clean the place is? Thanks a lot!"

She didn't know what was going on in my head; all *she* experienced was my frustrated words rushing into the room after the dam of my heart broke loose. Her eyes looked stunned—*What just happened here?* She was the unfortunate victim of my fear of man. I *needed* her to praise me. I *needed* her to think that I was a great husband—and when she didn't, my pride lashed out like a cornered animal trying to survive.

To better understand the fear of man, we need to understand its origin. God created mankind in his image (see Gen. 1:26–27), which means that we were created to be in a relationship with God—to be a son or daughter of God—and to show the rest of creation what God is like as a Servant King. In the beginning, we found our identity, value, and significance in our relationship with God and in service to others. But when our first parents sinned in the garden, everything changed. The seriousness of their offense did not simply involve eating a piece of fruit; it involved a decision to reject God's rule over their lives out of a belief that things would be better if *they* were in charge. In effect, they replaced God with themselves at the center of creation. Thus, we have each inherited a nature that wants to put itself at the center—to seek *our* glory before God's.

But this self-centered worldview leaves us dependent on the opinions of others. Our value and identity no longer rest in the grace of being a child of God. Instead, they are based on how well we perform in comparison to others. A performance-based value system means that our value and significance are determined by what others think of us. No wonder our fear of others runs rampant in our relationships at home, school, work, and church. Now we *need* other people's approval to validate our identity and significance. We've become slaves to their opinions. So, how can we get back to paradise? How can we find the rest that comes from being children of God and the freedom that comes from serving others instead of using them to feel good about ourselves?

I wish I could tell you that I no longer struggle with the fear of man. The reality is that it's still a daily fight for me. But, after many years, I can say I have learned how to fight better. The fear that once screamed in my ear has become quieter and quieter. To overcome our fear of others, we must *understand* what it is, *identify* where it is in our lives, and *equip ourselves* with the tools God provides us for overcoming it.

If possible, read this book with a trusted friend, counselor, or pastor. Taking the time to reflect on and unpack what you're learning about God and your own heart is crucial to the process. So don't rush. Read, discuss, and pray that God would transform your heart and mind. David prays in Psalm 34:4, "I sought the LORD, and he answered me and delivered me from all my fears." My prayer for you, as you read this book, is that God would deliver *you* from all your fears.

UNDERSTAND AND IDENTIFY YOUR FEAR OF OTHERS

One of the purposes of surgery is to get rid of the disease that's attacking the body. When a doctor performs surgery, he or she must know *what* to look for and *where* the problem is. Our fight against fear of others involves "spiritual surgery" under the steady hands of Jesus, our Great Physician (see Mark 2:17). The aim of this first section is to help us understand how Scripture defines the fear of man and to help us identify it in our own lives. Once we know what it is and where to look for it, we can focus in the next session on overcoming our fear of others and rooting it out of our lives.

DAY 1

We Obey What We Fear

"Has the LORD as great delight in burnt offerings and sacrifices, as in
obeying the voice of the LORD? Behold, to obey is better than sacrifice, and
to listen than the fat of rams." . . . Saul said to Samuel, "I have sinned,
for I have transgressed the commandment of the LORD and your words,
because I feared the people and obeyed their voice." (1 Sam. 15:22, 24)

SAUL WAS ISRAEL'S first king. His inauguration marked a key
transition in the nation's history—even though he was reluctant
to accept the responsibility and even tried to hide from it! But
God gave Saul his Spirit and promised him everything he needed
in order to rule well. All Saul had to do was to fear God and obey
his commands. If he did, God promised that "it will be well"
(1 Sam. 12:14). Not too far into his rule, God called Saul to war
against the Amalekites and told him to destroy everything. But
Saul kept the best of the livestock for himself and destroyed only
that which was worthless or of poor quality. This partial obedience was disobedience.

Saul's confession in 1 Samuel 15:24 shows us how the fear
of man works. Why did he disobey God? Because he "feared
the *people* and obeyed *their* voice." According to the Bible, fear
is more than feeling terrified. Our fear of man certainly includes
that, but it also means revering people, needing them, or valuing
their opinion *so much* that our decisions end up being controlled
by them. We obey what we fear. As a result, our fear of others is
a worship issue. Every human heart is always worshipping something; we were made for worship (see Isa. 43:7; John 4:20–24)!
The question is, *who* we are worshipping—God or people?

Sprite's slogan tells us, "Obey your thirst." This soft-drink
advertisement ends up being pretty theologically accurate. What

we value indicates what we fear losing or never achieving. We can't imagine living without it, so this fear directs our decisions and motivates us to act. Isn't this what happens when the sports enthusiast prioritizes watching his team above attending church? Don't we refuse to share the gospel with a friend because we fear how she'll respond? Aren't we reluctant to take risks for good things because we can't bear the thought of being a failure? We thirst for and value something more than God in these moments. We obey what we fear.

Reflect: What are the ways you are tempted to disobey God in order to gain or keep the favor of people?

Reflect: Jesus taught that "where your treasure is, there your heart will be also" (Matt. 6:21). Think about what you fear losing or never achieving. What do your fears reveal about what you value or worship?

Act: There are no tricks or shortcuts to overcoming our fear of others—it's hard work! We need the Spirit of God to help us taste and see the goodness and glory of God so that we desire him more. We see God in the pages of Scripture; we rely upon him by pouring our hearts out to him in prayer. All of God's Word shows us who he is, but if you're looking for a place to start, take some time to reflect on passages like Psalm 103, Isaiah 40:6–31, or Colossians 1:15–23. Then pray! Ask God to open your eyes. Ask him to help you taste and see his goodness and to change your heart to value him more.

DAY 2

Monument Building

Samuel rose early to meet Saul in the morning. And it was told Samuel,
"Saul came to Carmel, and behold, he set up a monument for himself
and turned and passed on and went down to Gilgal." . . . *Samuel said,*
"Though you are little in your own eyes, are you not the head of the tribes
of Israel? The LORD anointed you king over Israel." (1 Sam. 15:12, 17)

SAUL HAD A "little big man" complex. He was Israel's newly
appointed king—the hopes of the nation were on him, and he
wanted to deliver. Problem is, the work was more than Saul could
handle. When he looked to his *own* ability, he was "little" in his
own eyes. What if people found out that he didn't have what it
took? What if people were disappointed? He couldn't bear the
thought of being seen as a failure or exposed as being in over his
head. He was desperate for people to see him as *big*—as a king they
could rely on, who was wise, strong, successful, and impressive.

What was Saul to do? When he became king, God promised
to provide him with everything he needed in order to rule well.
All Saul had to do was trust God. Sounds simple, right? Israel's
king was designed to be a vassal king—to follow God's lead and
serve God's people for God's glory. The problem is that Saul didn't
like that setup. He didn't want to be in anyone's shadow (not even
God's)—Saul wanted the glory for himself. But when he pushed
God out of the picture, he was left to rule the nation with his own
resources. All this led to the "little big man" complex. How would
he keep up the facade that he was a big man? By building monuments for himself.

Saul's problem illustrates what fear of others can look like in
our lives. Monument building is a sign that we've fallen prey to
the fear of man. We may not build physical monuments, but we

have our own way of trying to garner the praise of man. There are times when I finish preaching and feel uncertain how it went. Was it clear? Were people strengthened by God's Word? Or was it a disaster? One Sunday, when I got in the car after church, I remember complaining to my wife, "Well, that was awful, wasn't it?" Why did I ask it *that* way? Because I hoped she would say, "Are you kidding? It was great! Why would you think it was awful, honey?!" Instead of trusting in God, I was fishing for compliments in order to build myself a monument. What about you?

Reflect: What's something God has called you to do that you're inadequate to do in *your* resources? Part of Saul's problem was an issue of identity: "The LORD anointed you king over Israel" (1 Sam. 15:17). When he anointed Saul, God promised to help him. God often calls us to do something that is beyond us, so that we trust him. As we do, our weakness becomes the stage for his strength.

Reflect: Are you guilty of monument building? Setting things up so that people will remember *you* and be impressed with *you*?

Act: Next time you are tempted to fish for compliments, remember that this isn't about you! Do your best, pray fervently, and trust God with the results. Take pleasure in the fact that God delights in using your weakness or inadequacy, for "when I am weak, then I am strong" (2 Cor. 12:10).

DAY 3

Watch Out! It's a Trap!

*The fear of man lays a snare, but whoever trusts
in the L*ORD *is safe. (Prov. 29:25)*

THE BEST FISHERMEN are good liars. Now, before any fishing
enthusiasts put the book down, let me explain. The goal of fishing
is to deceive—to convince the fish that we're offering a free meal,
not a concealed hook. This past summer I taught my two boys
this art of deception. After putting the nightcrawlers on the hook,
we dropped the line into the water and waited. One by one, the
fish approached the bait and thought, *How convenient! I can skip
the hard work of chasing lunch and eat this delicious worm, free of
charge* (at least, that's my best attempt at fish thinking). But what
seemed convenient was a snare. One by one, the deceived fish took
the bait and, instead of enjoying a meal, *became* our meal.

We often feel tempted to change our conduct, convictions,
or character out of panic. We fear what others may say about us,
what they may do to us, or what we might miss out on. Like the
fisherman's bait, the fear of man promises one thing but delivers
another. The temptation to fear whispers, *Compromising this once
won't do any harm. Join your friends in order to fit in; there's plenty of
time to do what God wants later. Facing the rejection of these friends
would be unbearable. Go ahead—God will forgive you.* But when we
cave to the temptation, we take the bait only to realize that we've
been deceived! Instead of delivering what it promised, our fear of
others leaves us ensnared by sin and suffering its consequences.

What's the alternative to the fear of man? Our proverb provides the answer through contrast. The alternative to "the fear of
man" is to "trust in the LORD." The alternative to being caught
in the "snare" is to find the freedom in being "safe." The word for

"safe" paints a picture of a person who is lifted above harm's reach, making him inaccessible to danger.[1] The fear of man makes this *promise* of deliverance, but only to conceal a hook that drags us to death. Only God delivers on every promise that he makes. Only God is worthy of our trust.

Reflect: When have you been ensnared or entangled in a mess because of your fear of others? Perhaps you are in that mess right now. What did your fear of others promise you that made changing your conduct, conviction, or character seem like a good idea in the moment?

Reflect: When have you, by God's grace, said no to fearing others and enjoyed the safety of trusting in God? How would you describe your experience before and after your decision to trust him?

Act: Once you identify ways that you tend to be ensnared by the fear of man, you may ask, "I'd love to trust God more— but how?" Proverbs 29:6 says, "An evil man is ensnared in his transgression, but a righteous man sings and rejoices." No one is righteous on his or her own. In that sense, we are all ensnared in our transgressions. But that's how and why we trust God. Our hope isn't in our righteousness. It's in Jesus, who willingly became ensnared in our sin so that we could sing and rejoice in the freedom of his righteousness. Next time you are tempted with the fear of man, remember its empty promises in contrast to the promises that Jesus has fulfilled for your salvation.

DAY 4

The Difficulty of Waiting

O my God, in you I trust; let me not be put to shame;
let not my enemies exult over me. Indeed, none who wait
for you shall be put to shame. (Ps. 25:2–3)

Isn't that a wonderful promise? *No one* who truly waits for God will *ever* be put to shame! If you trust God, there will *never* come a time when you'll look back with regret and think, *Boy, that was a mistake. God never came through on what he promised.* In the end, the one who waits on God will always confess, "God came through! I wasn't put to shame for trusting him! It was worth the wait!"

The problem is, waiting is difficult! Bumper-to-bumper traffic, slow checkout lines at the grocery store, the waiting room in the doctor's office —no one likes waiting. Our children say, out loud, what we often feel in our hearts: "Are we there yet?!" But trusting God in a fallen world often involves waiting. Abraham waited for twenty-five years before seeing the fulfillment of God's promise of a child (see Gen. 12:4; 21:5). God didn't part the Red Sea until the last minute, after the Egyptians had the Israelites surrounded and all hope seemed lost (see Ex. 14). The Christian waits for Christ's return (see Rev. 22:20) and for the redemption of our ailing bodies (see Rom. 8:23).

The basic posture of the Christian life is *waiting*.

Waiting is especially hard when disaster looms overhead, a deadline presses in, or a situation threatens our hope—when something needs to change, and soon! When disaster looms, it's tempting to give up waiting, take control of the steering wheel, and do it *our* way, not God's. As a result, waiting becomes a litmus test that reveals whom and what we fear—who or what controls us.

21

Will the opinions of others, or what they *might* do to me, drive my decision? Or will I wait patiently for God because I trust him and his promises? Remember, "*None* who wait for you shall be put to shame" (Ps. 25:3).

> **Reflect:** What are you waiting for? How does that put pressure on you to take a sinful shortcut?
>
> **Reflect:** Do you ever look at non-Christians with envy and think, *They don't have to wait on God; they can do what they want. Wouldn't that be nice?*
>
> **Act:** Waiting requires perspective. We need to be able to see the big picture. That's what Asaph models for us in Psalm 73. He envied the wicked in their apparent ease and prosperity (see v. 3) until he saw their end (see v. 17). What promise of God are you struggling to believe? Trace the promise to its end. Now compare it to the end of the path for those who trust themselves.
>
> **Act:** Thankfully, we aren't alone in finding it difficult to wait. The psalmist cried out to God, "How long?" on more than one occasion. The Psalms are a sort of prayer template—a tool we can use to help us pray as we wait on God. Take some time to read Psalm 13, and turn it into a prayer of your own.

DAY 5

Busy, Busy, Busy

"At the time for the banquet he sent his servant to say to those who had been invited, 'Come, for everything is now ready.' But they all alike began to make excuses. The first said to him, 'I have bought a field, and I must go out and see it. Please have me excused.' And another said, 'I have bought five yoke of oxen, and I go to examine them. Please have me excused.' And another said, 'I have married a wife, and therefore I cannot come.'" (Luke 14:17–20)

DO YOU EVER feel overcommitted? Spread too thin? A friend recently told me about the stress he is under at work. He has always worked hard, got his projects done, and been well respected at work. But recently his boss has demanded so much that he isn't sleeping well and comes home with a short fuse, sometimes blowing up over miniscule issues. As we talked about what drove him to work such long hours and to answer every call and email during his off-hours, the answer became clear: he didn't want to disappoint his boss. He'd earned the reputation of being the guy who *gets it done*. He was proud of it, and he didn't want things to change.

Being overcommitted can be a symptom of fearing others. Like my friend, you may find it difficult to say no to people because you're afraid of falling from the pedestal they have put you on in their minds. When this happens, being overcommitted isn't just an issue of priorities—your priorities are being driven by a *need* for people to think of you a certain way.

In Luke 14, the guests checked "not coming" on their invitation to the heavenly banquet because of a field, oxen, and a recent marriage. Some oxen or a field instead of *heaven*? What were they thinking?! The world wants to convince us that being wealthy, being famous, or drinking deeply from the world's pleasures is *most* important. When those commitments become habits that control our priorities, the things of God become unimportant to us.

One way to recalibrate our priorities and motivations is to reexamine our commitments through gospel lenses. The King of Kings has invited sinners like *us* to his banquet! There is no greater privilege or honor. When we remember who does the inviting and how unworthy we are to be his guests, oxen and fields (or anything else that we give priority to) don't look so important anymore. We see rightly that honoring God is infinitely more important than honoring man.

Reflect: Do people hold an opinion of you that you're proud of? Are there ways you are motivated out of fear that their opinion of you may change?

Reflect: At some point this week, ask a trusted friend for his or her perspective on your priorities. Would he say that you have trouble saying no and that you overcommit because of a fear of man? Is she aware of ways that you make excuses for doing good things at the expense of following God?

Act: Reflect on Paul's prayer in Philippians 1:9–11, and then take some time to prayerfully examine your calendar for the coming month. Pray that your commitments would be controlled by love for God and others—not by fear.

DAY 6

The Fear of Falling

*Jesus said to them, "I will ask you one question; answer me, and I
will tell you by what authority I do these things. Was the baptism of
John from heaven or from man? Answer me." And they discussed it
with one another, saying, "If we say, 'From heaven,' he will say, 'Why
then did you not believe him?' But shall we say, 'From man'?"—
they were afraid of the people, for they all held that John really was
a prophet. So they answered Jesus, "We do not know." And Jesus
said to them, "Neither will I tell you . . ." (Mark 11:29–33)*

THE FEAR OF heights is not always a matter of altitude. As Tim
Keller explains, "The higher a person climbs the greater the possibility of a terrible fall, for there is now so much to lose. When
Bernard Madoff was sentenced to 150 years in prison for run-
ning a $65 billion Ponzi scheme, he publicly blamed his pride. At
some time in the past he had faced a year in which he should have
reported significant losses, but he could not 'admit his failures
as a money manager.' He could not accept the loss of power and
reputation that such an admission would bring. Once he began to
hide his weaknesses through the Ponzi scheme, he then 'couldn't
admit his error in judgment while the scheme grew.' "[1]

When Jesus enters the temple in Mark 11, we see a similar
power struggle. Those who thought *they* were in charge (the chief
priests, scribes, and elders) had been threatened by Jesus's actions
in the temple the day beforehand. They came questioning his
authority, essentially asking, "Jesus, who do you think you are?
Don't you know *we're* in charge?"

In response, Jesus offered a counterquestion: "Was the baptism of John from God or from man?" When Jesus was baptized
by John, the heavens opened up and God the Father declared

Jesus to be his Son (see Mark 1:9–11). Jesus's baptism was a neon sign that inaugurated his divine authority. If the temple leaders wanted their question answered, they would need to rethink *John's* ministry. But "they were afraid of the people" (v. 32). Jesus's question had exposed their hearts. They were afraid that Jesus would take their place of honor and that they would lose the respect of the crowds.

How sad! Had they been willing to have *honest* dialogue, they might have learned who Jesus is. But they were *unwilling*. They were more interested in doing whatever it took to get *rid* of Jesus (who posed a threat to what they valued) than in finding the truth. For those who refuse to listen, Jesus refuses to speak.

Reflect: You don't need to suffer from the fear of heights to be afraid of falling. Like the religious leaders of Jesus's day, we too can fear falling from the pedestal we stand on in people's view of us. How might the fear of falling (of losing power, influence, or the respect of others) affect your decision making? What would it look like to trust God in those same decisions?

Act: If you are able to identify ways that you're afraid of falling, bring them into the light by sharing them with a trusted friend. Sometimes the best way to overcome our fear is to turn the lights on what we're thinking and to call our fear of man out for what it is.

DAY 7

The Surprising
Source of Confidence

*In the fear of the LORD one has strong confidence, and
his children will have a refuge. (Prov. 14:26)*

TRUE CONFIDENCE COMES through fear.

Such a statement sounds puzzling at first, because we assume
that confidence comes from competence. But even the most
self-reliant, self-made, gifted individuals lack *true* confidence
without the fear of God. They may display a confident bravado
on the outside, but inside they are shaking in their boots. They're
afraid the things that make them confident (their gifts, abilities,
and strengths) will be taken away or will soon deteriorate. If they
are no longer able to sing, no longer beautiful, no longer able to
work, no longer wealthy, what will they do? Proverbs teaches that
true confidence is found not in competency but in fearing the
right person. Oswald Chambers was right: "The remarkable thing
about fearing God is that when you fear God, you fear nothing
else, whereas if you do not fear God, you fear everything else."[1]

Fearing God does not mean dreading evil from him. There *is* a
knee-knocking, jaw-dropping vulnerability that we get from coming into contact with the God of the Bible. But, far from being
evil, he is *good*. The same power of God that makes us tremble is
the power that's available to protect the child of God.

When you're in third grade, the playground bully is frightening—until Dad shows up. In the same way, if you fear God,
everything else that *could* frighten you is puny compared to an
almighty God. If God is on your side, you can walk through the
valley of death but remain safe and sound. That's why the children

of God-fearers *have a refuge*. God is far better than any home security system that money can buy.

I pray Proverbs 14:26 for my two sons every week. I want them to be confident, but not cocky. The difference between the two comes from whom we fear. You can't see God in his glory and be cocky. But when we see God for who he is, we gain a profound confidence from a profound refuge.

Reflect: What do you fear most: the potential consequences of obedience, or disobeying God?

Reflect: Proverbs 14:26 teaches that fearing God provides confidence for the individual and a refuge for his or her children. Our children (and others whom we influence) learn from our examples, not just from our words. Do you model what it means to fear God in humble obedience? Do you prove the promises of God's Word through your actions as well as your words?

Act: The next time you're afraid of losing the thing that your confidence rests in, shift your focus from your abilities to God's character. To see God's character, meditate on his Word—on texts like Job 38, Psalm 34, or Mark 5–6. As you read, ask God to open your eyes to see his greatness so that you will find true confidence in fearing him.

DAY 8

Confidence in Your Insufficiency

Such is the confidence that we have through Christ toward God.
Not that we are sufficient in ourselves to claim anything as coming
from us, but our sufficiency is from God. (2 Cor. 3:4–5)

IT'S A DELIGHT watching children discover the world around
them and acquire new skills: brushing teeth, tying shoelaces, or
learning to read on their own. Once the skill is mastered, a child
loves to show what they've learned: "Look! Watch! I can do it
myself!" As children grow, independence is a sign of health and
maturity. But when in our relationship with God, maturity is
measured by *dependency* on God, not *independence.*

As a minister of the gospel, Paul understood this. Under the
old covenant, the law of God showed people what was good,
but offered no help for the hearer when it came to obedience.
Thankfully, God had promised his people long ago, "I will give
you a new heart, and a new spirit I will put within you. And I
will remove the heart of stone from your flesh and give you a
heart of flesh. And I will put my Spirit within you, and cause
you to walk in my statutes" (Ezek. 36:26–27). When Christ
ushered in the new covenant, this promise was fulfilled! As Paul
preached, he found confidence in knowing the Holy Spirit does
the work in the heart of the hearer. Paul himself *was* inadequate,
but the more he relied on God, the more he *was* sufficient for
the task.

My friend launched an internet company in Washington D.C.
but found the job led to unbearable worry. What if the company
failed to deliver on a project and a client canceled? How could
they replace a key employee leaving the company? What if they
ran out of money and went out of business? Worry filled his mind

as soon as he woke up. Before he left his room each morning, he felt defeated.

This went on for years—until one day, he decided to *actively* bring his worry to God. Each morning, he began taking walks to rehearse biblical truths and pour out his concern to God in prayer. Before long, hope returned, not because the challenges disappeared, but because *he* was changed. God had begun to heal him of his crippling fear of failure.

Fear of failure is one manifestation of fearing others. We assume the *results* of a God-given task are up to us, and panic. But like my friend, the more we rely on God (not our self), the more we'll be free to work hard, do our best, and trust God with the results.

Reflect: Paul knew his adequacy rested not in his sufficiency but in relying on an all-sufficient God. What about you? What has God called you to do that seems impossible? A spouse you need to forgive? A sin you need to conquer? A neighbor you need to evangelize? A job you need to be faithful in? A friend you need to confront?

Act: How should we respond when we fear failure in a God-given task? Spirit-empowered obedience includes five steps. 1) Admit the truth: apart from God, you can't do this. 2) Pray and ask God for the strength, wisdom, and grace you need. 3) Trust God's promises of help, strength and guidance. 4) Act in obedience, stepping in into the responsibility God calls you into from Scripture. 5) Thank God for his help to do what you could not apart from his help.[1]

DAY 9

The Grasshopper Syndrome

"We are not able to go up against the people, for they are stronger than we are.... The land, through which we have gone to spy it out, is a land that devours its inhabitants, and all the people that we saw in it are of great height. And there we saw the Nephilim ... and we seemed to ourselves like grasshoppers." (Num. 13:31–33)

GOD HAD PROMISED to bring his people into the land flowing with milk and honey. During the exodus, he proved that no obstacle can frustrate his plan and that he is faithful to keep his promise. "Our God is in the heavens," the psalmist says; "he does all that he pleases" (Ps. 115:3). And yet, when the twelve spies went into Canaan, they found the people so big that they felt like grasshoppers! Based on this information, taking the land seemed impossible. It's a reminder that what we fear controls us. For the spies, it was the Canaanites. In fact, they were ready to go back to Egypt—the place where they'd been brutally enslaved for almost four hundred years!

God wanted his people in the promised land, so why did he send spies in the first place? It's not as if *God* needed the information they would gather. If the spies never went in, they might have avoided this fear. Better yet, God could have removed the people from the land before they arrived. Why do it *this* way?

God knew that Israel was outmatched and didn't stand a chance in their own strength. But *they* needed to know that God was bigger than the people who made them feel small. In other words, God wants his people to trust him.

My youngest son is still learning to swim, but he enjoys jumping into the deep end when someone is there to catch him. Imagine that I'm in the pool and I tell him, "Son, jump! I *promise*

31

I'll catch you"—only to have him look at me and say, "Dad, I *want* to jump, but there's no way you'll catch me. I'll pass." Is he *honoring* me? No! He honors me by launching himself into the pool, confident that I'll catch him. In the same way, we glorify God when we trust him.

Oswald Chambers once said, "God can achieve his purpose either through the absence of human power and resources, or the abandonment of reliance on them. All through history God has chosen and used nobodies, because their unusual dependence on him made possible the unique display of his power and grace. He chose and used somebodies—only when they renounced dependence on their own natural abilities and resources."[1]

Reflect: What circumstances are you dealing with that make obedience to God frightening? How might those circumstances be an *opportunity* for you to trust God?

Reflect: Sometimes we wrongly assume that God uses only the people who are bright, gifted, and strong. As Oswald Chambers reminds us, God uses our weakness as the platform on which to display his strength (see 2 Cor. 12:9–10). What hope does that offer you in your situation?

Act: The spies were paralyzed by fear because they saw people as big and God as small. For every glance we take at the people we fear, we need to take two glances at God in order to remember who he is. Next time you are tempted to fear, make a list with two columns: one to catalogue your concerns, and the other to remind yourself of who God is and what he has promised. Having trouble remembering? Ask a godly friend to help you write the list with an open Bible.

DAY 10

Keeping People at a Distance

The eye cannot say to the hand, "I have no need of you," nor again the head to the feet, "I have no need of you." (1 Cor. 12:21)

SINCE THE FEAR of man shows itself in our need for people to like us or to think a certain way of us, we may assume that *not* needing anyone means that we *don't* fear man. But is that true? Consider four types of people:

- *The tough guy.* It seems like nothing could rattle him. He'll serve others, but he finds it hard to *be* served lest he be in a position of needing someone. Cool and calm, he *appears* to have it together. Yet when it comes to relationships, "tough guys" keep people at a distance. They may talk, but they never open their hearts to their friends, kids, or spouses.
- *The noncommittal.* She loves the "maybe" option on an invitation. Allergic to the idea of making a commitment, she is fine with hanging out—as long as she can keep her options open. If things get too close or uncomfortable, she wants the option of taking the exit door.
- *The risk-avoider.* Whether he's been hurt in the past or fears the possibility of it happening in the future, he rarely initiates a relationship, invites someone over, or starts a conversation. When he does talk, he sticks to the safe topics: weather, sports, or what he saw on TV.
- *The pretender.* Ask how she's doing, and her answer is always "Great"—even if, inside, she is dying. Perhaps her job is at risk or a relationship is crumbling. It could be unconfessed sin that is eating away at her (see Ps. 32:3–4). Whatever the

cause, she feels safer keeping it close to the chest rather than letting someone see her this way.

What do these people all have in common? They may look different, but they're all saying the same thing: *I can do this on my own. It's safer if I do it alone.* Don't be deceived! Strength and confidence aren't defined by being independent or not needing anyone. As Paul reminds us in 1 Corinthians 12, we *can't* say that we have no need of others. As the body of Christ, we were created by God to rely on each other. True confidence is being able to open our hearts, be vulnerable, and accept the risks.

Reflect: Are there people who really know you? Not what you put on your resume or social media profile, but your hopes and dreams, successes and failures, faith and fears?

Reflect: You can be everyone's friend and yet be known by no one (see Prov. 18:24). You can isolate yourself (see Prov. 18:1). There are many ways that fear motivates us to keep people at a distance. How are you tempted to push people away?

Act: Are you a member of the church you attend? If you're new to an area and are trying to look for a good church, looking around is understandable. But at some point, it's good to stop church-shopping and join! Making that commitment is a good way to fight the fear of man and to promise to love others and be known by them. If there are ways that people in the church have offered to serve you but you have refused because of pride and fear, take them up on it and thank them for their help.

DAY 11

Don't Take It Personally

The vexation of a fool is known at once, but the
prudent ignores an insult. (Prov. 12:16)

Wife: "Honey, you were supposed to turn left back there."
Me: "*No*—this is a shortcut. (. . . *I hope!*)"
Wife: "Babe, it's icy; maybe you should slow down."
Me: "Hmph! I know how to drive." [*said under my breath*]

I love and respect my wife—so why are there times I get
defensive or snap at her when she tells me how to drive? It's
because I'm convinced that I *am* a good driver! Inside my heart,
I'm thinking, *Don't you know who I am? Mario Andretti has nothing
on me!*

Often we take offense to things people say because we believe
I'm right; I'm better; I'm more important; I'm more valuable. We
may not say that out loud, but our high thoughts about ourselves
are a defensive attempt for us to save face—to make sure that people see us as being as important, as beautiful, as skilled, as strong
as we think we are. Are you easily embarrassed? Are you often
offended and defensive? Chances are, it's because the fear of man
is in your heart.

"The vexation of a fool is known at once," Proverbs tells us.
The word *vexation* describes an agitated, provoked, stirred-up,
emotionally volatile state of heart.[1] Feeling upset when you feel
insulted is *not* the problem that Proverbs condemns. The problem
is that the vexation is "known at once." The fool speaks and *then*
thinks.

The prudent, we are told, "ignores an insult." It's not that prudent people pretend that insults don't happen. Instead they cool

down, pray about it, and *then* respond. How can they do that? Those who fear man are controlled by what others think of them, so when their image is threatened their knee-jerk reaction is to defend that image as if their life depended on it. But those who fear God can ignore an insult or assume the best in the offender. They understand that the most important thing is not what others think about *them* but about *God*. No wonder Proverbs teaches us that the fear of the Lord is the beginning of wisdom (see Prov. 1:7; 9:10)!

Reflect: Are you defensive when a friend confronts your sin? Do you immediately deny it or turn on them and talk about their sin? Do you feel slighted when you're not noticed at school? When you're not recognized or thanked? How do you respond when you are wronged? When you feel disrespected or insulted? Part of knowing how to respond rightly is recognizing when we tend to respond wrongly.

Act: How much of our defensiveness would vanish if we walked into the room in order to serve rather than to be seen as important! Next time you are tempted with defensiveness, remember Christ's example: "When he was reviled, he did not revile in return; when he suffered, he did not threaten, but continued entrusting himself to him who judges justly" (1 Peter 2:23). Remembering that he did this to "[bear] our sins in his body" (v. 24) goes a long way toward helping us to entrust ourselves to God instead of feeling the need to defend ourselves.

DAY 12

You Shall Not Covet

Let not your heart envy sinners, but continue in the fear
of the LORD all the day. Surely there is a future, and
your hope will not be cut off. (Prov. 23:17–18)

WHILE I WAS listening to the radio this past week, an advertisement about men's hair loss came on the air, saying, "Hair is
the most important thing to a man! It's more important than
his looks, more important than his wallet—it's more important
than *anything.*" Whoa there! I understand that losing hair can be
tough—but *more important than anything*? Aren't we going a little
over the top to sell this product?

One of the tools an effective advertisement can use to sell a
product is to exploit fear. Exaggerate our need for what they're
selling (a hair-loss product, clothing, food, a beverage, a course
on how to make money, and so on), and we fear the nightmare of
what life would be like *without* it. Buying their product becomes a
"mail-order savior" that we trust in to make us happy, whole, and
significant.

Envy works much like a fearmongering ad campaign. Envy
makes us believe that we *have* to have something. It convinces us
that if we don't have the same lifestyle, dress size, full head of hair,
gifting or ability, notoriety, or comfortable lifestyle that others
enjoy, we will *never* be happy, whole, or significant. Before long,
acquiring whatever it is controls our life. We think about it *all the
time*—how to get it, protect it, show it off, or find more of it.

Do you see how envy and fear are related? Proverbs 23:17
contrasts the two: "Let not your heart *envy* sinners, but continue in the *fear* of the LORD all the day." To envy others is to fear
them—to be controlled by the fear that we will never find what

will make us happy. To fear that we'll lose it if we *do* acquire it. The opposite of envy is to fear the Lord. The fear of the Lord sets us free from slavery to fear, because our hope is no longer in the *product* but in God. We entrust our future, value, and happiness to him! For those who fear God, "surely there is a future, and your hope will not be cut off" (Prov. 23:18).

Reflect: Envy is the resentment we feel when other people have what we want or think we deserve. Envy creates sorrow over others having what we do not.[1] Where does envy show up in your life? What are you hoping in and trusting for happiness or significance other than God?

Act: One of the best ways to combat envy is to pray for God to bless those whom we envy. It's hard to resent the person you are asking God to use, encourage, and grow. Take some time to pray for those whom you envy today and for God to replace envy in your own heart with the fear of the Lord.

Act: The fear of others that expresses itself in envy has a perspective problem. In Psalm 73, Asaph envied the prosperity of the wicked, until he stepped back and saw the big picture. When he "discerned their end" (v. 17), the easy life of the wicked didn't look so appealing. To fight envy, reflect on the future that God has promised you because you are in Christ.

OVERCOME YOUR FEAR OF OTHERS

Insecurity, fishing for compliments, impatience over waiting, overcommitting, never committing for fear of failure, keeping people at a distance, defensiveness, envy, pride . . . the symptoms that point to the fear of man are all around us. Once we understand how Scripture defines fearing others, we begin to see how much we *are* controlled by others. We see how miserable fearing others can leave us. So now that we see it, what can we do? How does God help us to put the sin of fearing others to death so that we can live (see Rom. 8:13)? In this second section, we turn our attention to the tools that Scripture gives us to fear God and not man.

DAY 13

Overcome Your Fear of
Others by Fearing God

"I tell you, my friends, do not fear those who kill the body, and
after that have nothing more that they can do. But I will warn you
whom to fear: fear him who, after he has killed, has authority to
cast into hell. Yes, I tell you, fear him! Are not five sparrows sold
for two pennies? And not one of them is forgotten before God.
Why, even the hairs of your head are all numbered. Fear not;
you are of more value than many sparrows." (Luke 12:4–7)

DEATH CAN BE a scary thing—it's the great unknown. But
Jesus teaches that there's something worse than death! The reality
of hell puts things into perspective. Our hope of overcoming the
fear of man doesn't rest in gimmicks but in fearing God *instead* of
man. Fearing God isn't like cowering under oppression or cruelty.
The fear of God is a reverence that trembles at his transcendence,
limitless power, and perfect justice.

When God revealed himself to Moses in the Old Testament,
he declared that he forgives "iniquity and transgression and sin."
Then he goes on to say, *"but* [he] will by no means clear the guilty"
(Ex. 34:7). Well now, that's a problem for sinners like us! A good
and just God will not wink at sin or sweep it under the carpet; he
will punish all sin—including yours and mine.

Let that sink in a bit. Hell, the place of weeping and gnash-
ing of teeth (see Luke 13:28) and eternal fire (see Matt. 25:41),
is what we deserve. Moreover, God "has authority to cast into
hell" (Luke 12:5). The good news of Christianity is not that God
ignores the demands of justice but that he pays our debt for us.
That's how a holy God can forgive sin. Christ himself bore our

sins in his body on the tree (see 1 Peter 2:24), and three days later he rose from the dead as proof that the debt was paid in full.

As Tim Keller writes, "The gospel is this: We are more sinful and flawed in ourselves than we ever dared believe, yet at the very same time we are more loved and accepted in Jesus Christ than we ever dared hope."[1] To overcome our fear of others, we need to grasp *both* these realities. When we rightly fear God as holy and transcendent, we realize how silly our fear of others is. When we see the depth of God's love and mercy, the approval of man that we long for is tawdry in comparison. Which of your fears should melt away in the light of God's greatness, mercy, and love?

Reflect: No problem compares to the problem of being at odds with God. The opinion of man will last for a season, but hell is forever. A Christian recognizes his or her sin and turns from it in order to trust in Jesus as Lord and Savior. Are you trusting in Christ today? If not, this is the starting point. Take time to pray—admit your need for him, confess your sin, and trust in Jesus. God promises that all who call on him in faith go from being at odds with him to being on his side. As the psalmist says, "The LORD is on my side; I will not fear. What can man do to me?" (Ps. 118:6).

Reflect: Luke 12:7 tells us to "fear not; you are of more value than many sparrows." The gospel reminds us how much God cares for us—enough that the Son of God would lay down his life for us. Do you believe that God loves you? Are you resting in that truth?

Act: Take a moment to thank God for his care and to pray for a greater comprehension of his love.

DAY 14

Fan the Flame

For this reason I remind you to fan into flame the gift of God, which is in you through the laying on of my hands, for God gave us a spirit not of fear but of power and love and self-control. (2 Tim. 1:6–7)

IN JULY OF 1505, Martin Luther was a young law student walking back to his German university when he was caught in a thunderstorm. Before he arrived at home, a lightning bolt struck so close that it knocked him to the ground. The reality of death sobered him, and in fear he cried out, "Saint Anne, help me! I shall become a monk!" True to his vow, he dropped out of law school and joined a monastery in the hope of finding refuge from the fear of death.

Fast forward fifteen years, and we find a different man. No longer cowering in fear, Luther stepped into a key leadership role in the Protestant Reformation. We find him a courageous man standing before a council for the sake of the gospel. With the wrath of the Holy Roman Emperor looming overhead, as well as the threat of being burned at the stake unless he recant his teachings, Luther responded, "I must walk in the fear of the Lord . . . my conscience is captive to the Word of God. I cannot and will not recant anything, since it is neither safe nor right to go against conscience. Here I stand. I can do no other."[1]

We may never face a dramatic, Luther-like stand, but the transformation that Luther experienced is true of *every* Christian. Paul describes this change in his encouragement to a young, timidity-prone pastor named Timothy. Take a moment to reread our text for today. In our battle against fear, we may be tempted to think, *That's just who I am,* and to give in to fear and anxiety. But that's *not* who you are! If you are in Christ, you are a new creation!

God has *not* given you a spirit of fear, but of courage—*powerful* courage, *loving* courage, and *self-controlled* courage.

The picture that Paul uses for this God-given courage is a flame. When we don't *feel* courageous, believing the truth about who God says we are can be difficult—as if the wick of our courage is about to be snuffed out. We fan the faint ember of courage into a roaring fire by poring over God's Word. It's here that we see God's character and how *big* he is. Soon, our courage blazes again.

Reflect: How do you see yourself? Do you let feelings, circumstances, and fear define your identity? Or, as Paul encourages you, do you let God's Word define what's true about you?

Reflect: In his book *The Unquenchable Flame*, Michael Reeves explains how Luther fanned his God-given courage into flame: "He battled his doubts by writing a relevant Bible verse on his wall, on a piece of furniture, or, indeed, on anything to hand. . . . He knew that within himself there was only sin and doubt. All his hope lay outside himself, in God's word. There his security before God was unaffected by how he felt or how he did. And so, when facing doubt, he would not look within himself for any comfort . . . instead, he would hold before his eyes this unchanging, external word."[2]

Act: One way to make sure that we fix our eyes on God's Word is by memorizing Scripture. Memorization helps us to hide God's Word in our hearts so that, wherever we are, we can quickly call it to mind. Need a place to start? Commit 2 Timothy 1:6–7 to memory.

DAY 15

Remember That God
Is Mindful of You

*When I look at your heavens, the work of your fingers, the moon and
the stars, which you have set in place, what is man that you are mindful
of him, and the son of man that you care for him? (Ps. 8:3–4)*

I HAD THE perfect solution to a perplexing problem. I was
one of several pastors at a church in Chicago who were sitting
in a staff brainstorming session. The solution was clear to me, so
once I got everyone's attention, I assumed that I'd share my idea,
that everyone would thank me, and that we'd put it into practice.
Problem solved. But I didn't get the response I expected. As soon
as I finished speaking, the group asked, "Any *other* ideas?" My
"brilliant" solution was tossed in the garbage, the meeting moved
on without skipping a beat, and they went with someone else's
idea. Being the mature, veteran pastor that I was, I knew just what
to do. I started to sulk, wallow in self-pity, and shut down. If they
didn't know a good idea when they saw one, I wasn't going to
speak up anymore.

By God's grace, I had read Psalm 8 during my devotions that
morning. As I sat there pouting, God kindly brought the psalm
to mind: "When I look at your heavens, the work of your fingers,
the moon and the stars, which you have set in place, what is man
that you are mindful of him?" It was as if God was saying, "Zach,
you're sulking because you're so desperate for the people in this
meeting to be mindful of you. Meanwhile, as the creator of the
heavens and the earth, *I* am mindful of you. Is that not enough?
Have you so quickly forgotten?"

It was *more* than enough. Since God is mindful of me, my

value no longer depends on the opinions of others. It is secure in the unmerited, gracious love of God! By reminding me of that truth, God pulled me out of my pity party, and I was able to reengage in the meeting. Free from worrying about myself, I was now free to care about God's name and the well-being of others.

As one who is made in the image of God and redeemed by the blood of Christ, you can rest assured that God is mindful of you. He is not distracted, too busy, or indifferent to you. Knowing who God is, and that he cares for you the way he does, makes all the difference.

Reflect: Whose approval are you desperate to gain? Is there someone who, if you had their admiration, attention, or respect, would make you content? How has the pursuit of this person's attention affected you?

Act: To enjoy the freedom that comes from God being mindful of us, we must remember, first, how great God is, and second, how much he cares. Take some time to reflect on each of these truths by reflecting on the following passages:

- the greatness of God—Isaiah 40:26; Isaiah 55:9; Jeremiah 32:17; Romans 11:33–36
- God's care for us—Psalm 121:5–6; Zephaniah 3:17; Luke 12:7; Romans 5:8

DAY 16

Relax; You're Not the Expert on You

*Search me, O God, and know my heart! Try me and know
my thoughts! And see if there be any grievous way in me,
and lead me in the way everlasting! (Ps. 139:23–24)*

THINK FOR A moment about the nature of introspection—
putting yourself on the examination table, under a spotlight, to
think about *you*. Some introspection is healthy. We look in the
mirror to assess how we're doing in terms of loving God, loving others, and fighting sin. But if we think about ourselves for
too long, we begin to view life with *self* at the center. Such self-
obsession is a bridge to fearing others. If we put ourselves at the
center, we stop seeing others as people whom we are to serve.
Instead, we ask, "What do they think about *me*? Do they like *me*?
How does this relationship benefit *me*?"

The Bible calls us to keep our hearts (see Prov. 4:23), to
examine ourselves to see whether we're in the faith (see 2 Cor.
13:5), and to examine ourselves before taking the Lord's Supper (1 Cor. 11:28). Self-examination is designed to help us to
trust God and keep sin's deception from hardening our hearts.
But sometimes we can be *so* introspective that we turn the tool
of self-examination into an idol. In other words, we depend on
self-knowledge in order to be "okay," rather than on God!

That's one thing that Psalm 139 can help us to realize. As the
one who created you (vv. 13–15) and is with you at all times (vv.
7–12), *God* is the expert on you. As a result, you don't have to
carry around the burden of knowing *everything* that's going on in
your heart. Yes, keep your heart and take time to examine yourself, but entrust yourself to him who knows you perfectly—and
rest. Instead of trying to be an all-knowing god, pray as David

does: "Search me, O God, and know my heart! Try me and know my thoughts!" Then trust the God who knows and loves you to lead you "in the way everlasting."

Reflect: When we ask a trusted friend or family member to help us, we stop worrying because we believe that person is competent and trustworthy and loves us. When we, like David, ask God to search our hearts and to lead us, how much more should we be able to pray and rest? Prayers like this don't obligate God to do our bidding, but they remind us that Christians are in a relationship with the living God who is all powerful and perfectly trustworthy and who loves us more than we can imagine (see Eph. 3:18–19). Can you trust that God loves you enough to use his people and his Word to point out your blind spots and lead you in the right direction?

Act: Are you at risk of being excessively introspective? If so, the next time you find yourself falling into that danger, take yourself off of introspection's examination table and ask, "How can I serve the people around me? What needs do they have that I can care for today?" That practical step of caring for others can be a declaration that you trust God to take care of you and to lead you in the way everlasting.

Take the Leap of Obedience

"Whoever has my commandments and keeps them, he it is who loves me. And he who loves me will be loved by my Father, and I will love him and manifest myself to him." (John 14:21)

BECOMING A PASTOR wasn't the *safe* option. I was in my final year at the University of Nebraska, studying to be a mechanical engineer, and the plan had always been to find a job after college and settle in. But after months of prayer and the encouragement of my church, I felt that God was calling me to the pastorate. The decision to follow his call was exciting, but it came with fears. How was I going to pay for seminary? What if I spent a lot of time and energy only to fail? Was I *actually* being called, or just being naive? I wanted God to lay out a divine five-year plan guaranteeing how things were going to happen, but it never came. There were no guarantees—only the command to trust God (see Prov. 3:5–6).

I made that decision fifteen years ago, and God has been faithful, walking with me and my family through ups and downs each step of the way. I would never have experienced God's help in the joys, sorrows, victories, and disappointments of pastoral ministry if he hadn't given me the grace to trust him. He gently and firmly pushed me out of my comfort zone and led me to say, "I don't know what the next five years or five minutes have in store for me, but I'm going to step out and trust God with this." I'm so thankful he did!

Sometimes the best approach to putting the fear of man to death is to take a step of obedience. God doesn't promise to give us grace five hours or five minutes ahead of time; he promises to give us mercy and grace to help *in time of need* (Heb. 4:16).

That's why Jesus says in John 14:21, "Whoever has my commandments and keeps them, he it is who loves me." Loving Jesus involves trusting him to keep his promises. The more we trust him and step out in obedience, the more we experience God's grace and faithfulness. As Jesus says in that same verse, "I will love him and manifest myself to him."

Maybe you've *heard* that God is powerful, wise, and faithful. We go from *hearing* these truths to *seeing* them ourselves when we trust and obey. It's then that God shows himself to be powerful, wise, and faithful. Seeing God with eyes of faith magnifies him, making the fear of man silly and the fear of God sensible.

Reflect: Do you want to see more of God? Is it possible that the reason you're not seeing him is because you're not trusting him in some area?

Act: Has fearing others kept you from stepping out in obedience? From sharing the gospel with a friend? From telling the truth in a precarious situation? From being generous when money is tight? From taking the risk of opening up in a relationship? Today, resolve to trust and obey God in what he asks of you. If risk prompts fear in your heart, fight fear with love, because obedience is an expression of love for God.

DAY 18

Redefine True Greatness

When the ten heard it, they began to be indignant at James and John.
And Jesus . . . said to them, ". . . Whoever would be great among you
must be your servant, and whoever would be first among you must
be slave of all. For even the Son of Man came not to be served but to
serve, and to give his life as a ransom for many." (Mark 10:41–45)

JAMES AND JOHN had just approached Jesus, trying to work a
back-alley deal. They wanted to be Jesus's number one and number two—his prime minister and chief of staff in the kingdom
of God. Their request to sit at Jesus's right and left was a grasp
at greatness; they wanted to make sure they'd be seen as *greater*
than the other disciples. But when the other ten found out, they
were indignant! So much of our discouragement, anxiety, and
fear originate from our concern about status: how do others see
me? How do they compare me to others? How do I measure up?
Do I fit in? Am I seen as important? But defining greatness by
comparison leaves us on a roller coaster. We fall into pride when
we're recognized and into despair when we're overlooked or
insulted. We lose sleep over *hoping* to gain respect and applause;
but when we gain it, we lose sleep over *fearing* that we'll fall from
the pedestal.

The world tells us that the path to greatness depends on
competition. We must prove ourselves *better* than others. It's not
enough to be faithful or good at something; we need to be *more*
intelligent, beautiful, strong, eloquent, wealthy, successful, or
respected than others. But Jesus is clear that "it shall not be so
among you." He has a different path to greatness from the world's
approach: "whoever would be great among you must be your servant, and whoever would be first among you must be slave of all"

(Mark 10:43). Isn't that interesting? Jesus doesn't condemn the pursuit of greatness. He redefines it and turns the world's definition and way of achieving greatness upside down.

Jesus says that the path to greatness is service—putting the interests of others before ourselves. Seeing them as more important than us. But that's tough—it feels risky! Pursuing greatness Jesus's way means throwing the world's way in the trash and going all in with Jesus's approach. So why take the "risk"? Jesus tells us why: "For even the Son of Man came not to be served but to serve, and to give his life as a ransom for many" (v. 45)

Do you see how silly we look when we flaunt our titles, achievements, and abilities next to the cross of Christ? The King, who deserves to be served, modeled true greatness for us by coming to serve sinners like us. What amazing love! Even in our unloveliness, Christ loved us and gave his life as a ransom for us. To know this love is to be set free from needing to compare ourselves to others in order to find significance. Jesus's sacrifice proves his love to our insecure hearts, so that now we have all the significance we need. We no longer need competition in order to prove our value—we have his grace.

Reflect: Think about the various positions you hold and the relationships you have. How can you use your different roles (as a boss, teacher, friend, and so on) to serve? What are ways you can serve your parents or siblings this coming week? What does it mean for you to be a servant as a husband or wife, a father or mother?

Act: Ask the Lord to help you make service, rather than comparison or competition, your greatest goal.

DAY 19

Know God's Purpose for Your Life

"Everyone who is called by my name, whom I created for
my glory, whom I formed and made." (Isa. 43:7)

YOU WERE CREATED to glorify God. As one who is made in
God's image, your purpose is to make God look good—to put
the spotlight on him and his beauty, goodness, righteousness, and
mercy. To live for any *other* purpose is to live like a fish out of
water; it leaves us discontent and longing for God. Ever since sin
entered the picture, we have managed to suppress the truth about
God and our need for him (see Rom. 1:18). We put ourselves in
the spotlight instead of God, and we live for *other* purposes, hoping that they will satisfy. But, as the third-century African theolo-
gian Augustine once said, "[God,] you made us with yourself as
our goal, and our heart is restless until it rests in you."[1] Living as if
we are the center, instead of God, creates and fuels a restless fear
of man.

The poet Emily Dickinson once said, of our search for the
spotlight, "Fame is a fickle food. . . . Men eat of it and die."[2] The
fickle nature of the spotlight feeds our fear of others in various
ways. Those who are desperate to be seen as important, beautiful, smart, or likeable find the target for achieving their notoriety
constantly moving. You work hard and give your time to pay your
entry fee into fame, only to see the criteria change. All that time
you spent—wasted! On the other hand, if you achieve success
and gain the spotlight, fear still haunts you because now there's
the chance that you'll *lose* it. No wonder Dickinson said, "Men eat
of it and die." Fame *is* a fickle food.

There is, however, a food that will satisfy and give life: knowing God and living for his glory. As Jesus said in John 6:35, "I

am the bread of life; whoever comes to me shall not hunger, and whoever believes in me shall never thirst." Living for his glory sets us free from fearing others, because our concern is no longer ourselves, but God. The criteria never changes, because it comes from his perfect Word. Far from being fickle, God's glory is a sure investment—no one will challenge God's purposes for his glory. As he has promised, "The earth will be filled with the knowledge of the glory of the LORD as the waters cover the sea" (Hab. 2:14).

Reflect: What are you living for? Comfort? Applause? Happiness that this world promises? The Westminster Shorter Catechism reminds us that "man's chief end is to glorify God and to enjoy him forever."[3] How would living for God's glory, instead of your own, make a difference in your fight against the fear of man?

Act: Take time to confess areas of your life in which you have put yourself at the center.

Act: We glorify God by trusting him (see Ps. 50:15). What are you trying to control that you need to trust God with? What are you carrying that you need to cast onto God's shoulders?

DAY 20

Embrace the Accusations

All who rely on works of the law are under a curse; for it is written,
"Cursed be everyone who does not abide by all things written in
the Book of the Law, and do them." ... *Christ redeemed us from*
the curse of the law by becoming a curse for us. (Gal. 3:10, 13)

BEING CRITICIZED ISN'T EASY. We like to be commended, complimented, and praised; but a criticism is a judgment about us, which shows how we fell short in some area. I see my own aversion to criticism in my defensiveness and pity parties, and I see it in other people, too. As a pastor, I've been in more than one counseling session in which someone tries to change the subject, blame others, or spin the scenario so as to lessen the blow of a criticism leveled against them. We know that a wise person listens to advice (see Prov. 12:15)—so why do we respond like this? Pastor Alfred Poirer explains: "We defend that which we deem of great value. We think it is our life we are saving. We believe something much larger will be lost if we do not use every means to rescue it. *Our name, our reputation, our honor, our glory.*"[1]

The fear of losing our glory, leading us to defend it at all costs, is another way that we fear man. How can we learn to respond well to criticism (like a wise person) instead of being devastated or defensive? By *embracing* the accusations. That's not to say we should make ourselves a punching bag—not every accusation is fair. But when we learn to see ourselves in light of the cross, we are able to accept criticism and learn from it. Think about what the cross says about us in our sin: "Cursed be everyone who does not abide by all things written in the Book of the Law, and do them" (Gal. 3:10). The truth is that the person who criticizes us sees only a tip of the iceberg of our sin. We didn't trust in Christ because we were good; we trusted in him because we knew our sinfulness and agreed with God's judgment of it.

The cross reminds us how sinful we are and how helpless we are to save ourselves, but it also reminds us how God makes sinners righteous. Paul tells us that "Christ redeemed us from the curse of the law by becoming a curse for us" (Gal. 3:13). That means that on the cross, Jesus took the punishment for the sin of *all* who repent and believe—and, in exchange, he clothes us with his perfect righteousness (see 2 Cor. 5:21). If that's how God justifies guilty sinners like you and me, we don't have to defend or justify ourselves against criticism. God knows *all* our sin, and he paid for it *all*. If we are accepted by God, we have nothing to fear—including criticism from others.

Reflect: How do you respond when you are criticized or corrected? Do you pout, blame, get defensive, shut down, or lash out? Many of the wrong ways that we respond are a subtle attempt to justify ourselves. In light of the cross, why are efforts aimed at our self-justification unnecessary?

Act: Take time to pray for God's help to be able to respond wisely to criticism and correction.

Act: The farther our minds drift from what Christ has done to save us, the harder it becomes for us to respond well to criticism. Take some time to reflect on the cross (for help, read Isaiah 53 or Romans 3). How can you not only know the truth of the cross but also live in light of it?

DAY 21

Fight Fear with Prayer

Do not be anxious about anything, but in everything by prayer and supplication with thanksgiving let your requests be made known to God. And the peace of God, which surpasses all understanding, will guard your hearts and your minds in Christ Jesus. (Phil. 4:6–7)

THE COMMAND IN Philippians 4:6 is clear: *do not be anxious—about anything.* Anything? Isn't that a little unreasonable? Doesn't he know about the test I have this week? The mortgage I have to pay? The speech I need to give? Doesn't he see the people I'm responsible for at home or at work? The temptations I'm facing? The sickness I'm dealing with? How does he expect me not to be anxious when all these things are uncertain? How can I *not* fear?

One reason for our worry is a lack of control. We fear what we can't control, and we hate feeling helpless. Worry seems useful, because it gives us the impression that we're doing something. But, in reality, we're not. When Jesus asks, "Which of you by being anxious can add a single hour to his span of life?" (Matt. 6:27), the answer is no one! Worry is only a *mirage* of being in control. Of course, some things that we fear *do* happen, but that doesn't make us prophets. Instead it shows that we use worry as a defense mechanism. We think, *Worry may make me miserable, but at least I'm ready for the worst.*

Instead of worrying, we're called to pray. What should we pray about? *Everything!* When should we pray? *Always.* Fear is the antithesis of faith, but prayer is the language of faith and of reliance on God. When we pray, we recognize that we *aren't* in control and commit the things we care about to the God who *is* in control. He gives good gifts to his children (see Matt. 7:11)

57

and delights to carry our burdens, because he cares for us (see 1 Peter 5:7). As H. B. Charles explains, "Prayer is arguably the most objective measurement of our dependence upon God. . . . The things you pray about are the things you trust God to handle. The things you neglect to pray about are the things you trust you can handle on your own."[1]

When prayer replaces fear, a beautiful thing happens: the peace of God, which surpasses all understanding, enters your life as a watchman. It guards your heart and mind from being overwhelmed by fear or anxiety.

Reflect: How much is your fear of man due to your desire to control circumstances, outcomes, opinions, or events?

Act: Sometimes the reason that we don't pray is because we doubt the goodness of God. Rather than waiting on him, we trust our definition of what's good and take matters into our own hands. To recalibrate your heart and mind on God's goodness, take a moment to remember these truths before you pray: God always gives good gifts to those who ask in prayer (see Matt. 7:11); God is generous (see Eph. 1:8; James 1:5); God delights to answer and provide, since it glorifies him as provider (see Ps. 50:15).

Act: Take time to pray about your circumstances and about the fear you are wrestling with in your heart. Be honest with God about what you feel and fear (see Ps. 62:8). Ask him to root out your fear of others in your life and to replace it with the fear of God (see Ps. 56:11). Thank God now for what he will do, as an expression of trust in God's wise and good answer (see 1 Thess. 1:2).

DAY 22

Look to Your Future Hope

The high priest asked him, "Are you the Christ, the Son of the Blessed?"
And Jesus said, "I am, and you will see the Son of Man seated at the right
hand of Power, and coming with the clouds of heaven."... As Peter was
below in the courtyard, one of the servant girls of the high priest came,
and... said, "You also were with the Nazarene, Jesus." But he denied it,
saying, "I neither know nor understand what you mean." And he went
out into the gateway and the rooster crowed. (Mark 14:61–62; 66–68)

MARK 14 RECORDS Jesus's trial before the Sanhedrin leading up to his crucifixion. Its focus is on the trial, but Mark arranges the story to highlight a contrast between Jesus's bold confidence and Peter's cowardly failure. The high priest's question was an exit ramp for Jesus (see v. 61). If Jesus denied the truth, he could skip the suffering of the cross and go free. But instead of caving to fear, he testified to the truth: he *is* the Son of God. When it was Peter's turn, he collapsed under fear and denied knowing the Son of God.

Why did Jesus succeed where Peter failed? Peter caved because his focus was so present tense that he lost sight of the future. Concerned about what people thought of him, he feared that the kingdom he had built on earth might crumble. He could lose his reputation, his belongings, his family, or his life. Our fear of others makes us vulnerable to temptation. It's not a menacing warlord with guns blazing that makes Peter cower—it's a little servant girl (see Mark 14:66). Three times he is questioned, and three times Peter denies Jesus. How tragic! Jesus bravely testifies that he's the Son of God for *Peter's* salvation, but Peter denies ever knowing Jesus.

In contrast, notice Jesus's answer back in verse 62: "You *will* see the Son of Man seated at the right hand of Power, and coming with the clouds of heaven." The title *Son of Man* comes from Daniel 7:13–14. It points to the future, when God will come again to judge the world and to right every wrong. Jesus's confidence is rooted in a *future hope*—they *will* one day see the Son of Man seated on the throne (see Ps. 110:1). Sure, he stands on trial before the Sanhedrin *now*, but the Sanhedrin will soon stand trial before the Son of Man when he returns in glory.[1] Jesus didn't cave to temptation, because he knew God's promise for the future and lived in the light of the hope it ensured. Sometimes what we need is to step back from our overwhelming circumstances and to remember the big picture that God guarantees for his children.

Reflect: When the things that we care about are at risk, that's where our attention goes. How are the circumstances of your life pressing in such that they block your view of the future that God promises?

Act: If, like Peter, you're ashamed about having been ashamed of Christ, remember the grace of God. Soon after this story, Jesus sought Peter out, restored him, and sent him back out (see John 21:17). Just as God's grace made Peter new, it can make you new. Peter would later write, "Rejoice insofar as you share Christ's sufferings, that you may also rejoice and be glad when his glory is revealed" (1 Peter 4:13). Take courage in your future hope!

DAY 23

Compete to Love, Not to Be Loved

*Love one another with brotherly affection. Outdo one
another in showing honor. . . . Rejoice with those who rejoice,
weep with those who weep. (Rom. 12:10, 15)*

DO YOU REJOICE when others succeed? It's easy to rejoice
in the success of someone who gets the silver medal, *if* you have
the gold medal around your neck. But it's hard to rejoice when
someone is on the platform and you're not. It's hard to rejoice
when your friend gets the promotion that you wanted, when
another couple in church gets pregnant but you and your spouse
cannot, when a peer gets into a school but you're left waiting,
when someone gets married and you're still looking. Though we
are called to rejoice with those who rejoice and weep with those
who weep, envy leads us to do the opposite. Envy rejoices when
others weep and weeps when others rejoice. No wonder "envy
makes the bones rot" (Prov. 14:30).

Envy and pride usually go together, with envy growing from
wounded pride. As C. S. Lewis wrote, "Pride is *essentially* com-
petitive. . . . Pride gets no pleasure out of having something, only
out of having more of it than the next man. We say that people
are proud of being rich, or clever, or good looking, but they are
not. They are proud of being richer, or cleverer, or better-looking
than others."[1]

A performance-based value system says that you're some-
body *if* people notice, praise, and appreciate how well you've
done. Those who live by such a value system are enslaved by their
fear of others. And no wonder! Their identity rests upon being
impressive. When I notice such envious fear of man in my heart,
I find it helpful to prayerfully switch gears: *God, I'm concerned*

about how I look to them; help me to be more concerned about loving them. Help me to serve them and work for their good, regardless of what they think of me. The competition that we *should* compete in is trying to out-serve and out-honor one another (see Rom. 12:10).

Reflect: Are you worried about whether others think you are smart, pretty, winsome, or gifted enough? Before or after you complete a task, do you find yourself more concerned with how people see you or with whether you're meeting their needs?

Act: It's hard to envy someone you're praying for. Take some time to pray for those whom you envy, asking God to bless, encourage, and use them.

Act: Jesus's command to love our neighbors as ourselves (see Mark 12:31) feels risky. If I love them, if I devote myself to pursuing their happiness, who is looking out for my happiness? The only way to give ourselves away in love (as Jesus calls us to do) is to first know God's love. That's why, before he commands us to love others, Jesus calls us to love God with all our heart, soul, mind, and strength (Mark 12:30). If you are struggling to love, out of fear over who is looking out for your happiness, take time to remember God's love for you in Christ and to rest in it. "God shows his love for us in that while we were still sinners, Christ died for us" (Rom. 5:8).

DAY 24

Know Who You Are

*This is how one should regard us, as servants of Christ and stewards
of the mysteries of God. Moreover, it is required of stewards that
they be found faithful. But with me it is a very small thing that I
should be judged by you or by any human court. In fact, I do not even
judge myself. . . . It is the Lord who judges me. (1 Cor. 4:1–4)*

WHEN YOU MEET someone for the first time, what's one of the
first questions that come up?

"What do *you* do?"

There's nothing wrong with asking people about their occu-
pation, but it does reflect our tendency to assign people value
based on the job or role that they play. We learn that someone is a
doctor, a plumber, a librarian, a pastor, a homemaker, or an engineer, or is looking for work. Then we put them in the appropriate
category, based on our culture's current economy.

One of the problems that Paul addresses in 1 Corinthians is
division in the church. The Corinthian believers were infected
with a celebrity culture, with one part of the church saying, "I follow Paul," while another said, "I follow Apollos." They assigned
value to different leaders based on their roles, leaving the church
divided (see 1 Cor. 3:3–4). But Christ, whom we follow, is not
divided (see 1 Cor. 1:13)! So, after reminding them that *God*
alone deserves the credit because he alone causes the growth (see
1 Cor. 3:7), Paul instructs his audience on how to view himself
and other teachers: as servants of Christ and as stewards. Servants
serve the agenda of their master; stewards manage what belongs
to others.

We may not be apostles like Paul, but we do well to imitate
his example here. You are more than your job. Fundamentally,

our value is rooted not in a role that we play but in our being made in the image of God (see Gen. 1:26–27). As image-bearers, we have the capacity (with God's help) to reflect what *God* is like in whatever role we play. In that sense, it doesn't so much matter whether I'm a lawyer, a table-waiter, or a counselor—what matters is *how* I practice law, wait on customers, or care for clients. Am I honest, fair, just, patient, loving, compassionate, and so on (see Gal. 5:22–23)? As stewards, we recognize that all we have has been given to us (see 1 Cor. 4:7). All that we have, all that we are, is not ours to use for *our* agenda or *our* glory. Our goal is to be faithful in serving God—to carry out *his* agenda, with *his* gifts, for *his* glory and the good of *others*. Knowing who you are can be very freeing.

Reflect: Where do you look for your value or significance? The more we look to our job for our identity, the more we become enslaved to our fear of others. It can feel like a very *big thing* to be evaluated by others. Look again at 1 Corinthians 4:3. Wouldn't it be freeing to say with Paul, "It is a very small thing that I should be judged by you or by any human court."

Act: Imagine yourself standing before God on the day of judgment. On *that* day, it will not matter what your colleague, classmate, neighbor, or friend thinks of you. What would it look like to serve others (as God would have you do) instead of to impress others? What would it look like to live faithfully today in the place where God has you? Take a moment to pray for God's help to live today in light of the final day. Ask God for an eternal perspective to see the opinion of others as a *small thing* and God's judgment as a *big thing*.

DAY 25

Fight Fear with Thankfulness

Let us come into his presence with thanksgiving; let us make a joyful noise to him with songs of praise! For the LORD is a great God, and a great King above all gods. In his hand are the depths of the earth; the heights of the mountains are his also. (Ps. 95:2–4)

ANNIE NO LONGER went to school, played with friends, or enjoyed the things that most twelve-year-old girls do.[1] Crippled by fear, she had reached a point at which the only place she felt safe was in her bedroom. It was remarkable that the little girl even went with her mom to talk to Paul David Tripp, a counselor working at the Christian Counseling & Educational Foundation. Annie was too afraid to talk during the first session, so in order to get to know the girl better, Tripp gave her an assignment. Over the next few weeks, she was to write down everything she was afraid of. When Annie brought back her completed homework, she had sectioned a paper into three columns, filling all three columns, front and back, with things she feared. She was afraid of *everything*—of life itself.

Overwhelmed, Tripp wasn't sure what to do. All Annie could see was what was wrong or what could go wrong. To help, he gave Annie and her mom a simple assignment: every night, she was to think of *one* thing from that day that she was thankful for. The first night, Annie couldn't think of anything—until, exasperated, she said, "You, Mom. I'm thankful for you sitting here with me." Annie's mom was the biggest picture of God that she had in her life, and that moment of thankfulness was a turning point. Slowly, she saw more and more things to give thanks for. After doing this exercise every night for months, Annie had so many things to give thanks for that it left her with a new problem: it kept her up past bedtime! Rather than looking around to find things to be afraid of, Annie was beginning to see God in her life. God was using thankfulness to drive out her fear.

Look again at our verse for today. It tells us, "Let us come into his presence with thanksgiving; let us make a joyful noise to him with songs of praise!" But *how* can we do this when the world seems to be falling apart? How can we do this when there's so much to be afraid of? Verses 3–4 give us the reason: "For the LORD is a great God, and a great King above all gods. In his hand are the depths of the earth; the heights of the mountains are his also." God *is* great. He *is* the King in control of your situation. From the deepest to the highest place you can go, everything is "in his hand." Thankfulness is a helpful way to see and remember what is true instead of believing the lies that feed our fear.

Reflect: In verses 7–11 of Psalm 95, the psalmist recalls how God's people complained at each step of his deliverance. As recovering complainers in a fallen world, we are like the Israelites in the wilderness—inclined to grumble. That means that thankfulness is an uphill climb. It takes effort and energy, but it's worth it!

Act: At the end of each day this week, take a moment to write down what you're thankful to God for. Share that list and discuss it with your spouse, kids, roommate, or friend. What are *they* thankful for?

DAY 26

Rejoice—God Is for You!

*If God is for us, who can be against us? He who did not spare his
own Son but gave him up for us all, how will he not also with
him graciously give us all things? . . . Who shall separate us from
the love of Christ? Shall tribulation, or distress, or persecution, or
famine, or nakedness, or danger, or sword? As it is written, "For
your sake we are being killed all the day long; we are regarded as
sheep to be slaughtered." No, in all these things we are more than
conquerors through him who loved us. (Rom. 8:31–32, 35–37)*

IN COLLEGE I helped to plan a six-week missions trip to east
Asia with eight other classmates. There was considerable prepara-
tion necessary in order for the trip to work. With all the moving
pieces involved—working full time, finishing my classes, trying
to pay for the trip and get a visa—I started to worry. The problem
wasn't the logistics, but that God seemed like he was out to get
me. I felt as if there was a dark cloud over everything and became
convinced that God was waiting for me to screw something up so
that he could teach me a lesson.

As I complained about this to my pastor at the time, his
response made all the difference. "Zach, you've got it wrong.
You're acting like God's against you, but he's proven his heart for
you a long time ago." Opening his Bible, he read Romans 8:32:
"He who did not spare his own Son but gave him up for us all,
how will he not also with him graciously give us all things?"

"Zach," he said, "what more could God do to show you his
love? I don't know what will happen. Maybe things *won't* work
out—but whatever happens will come from a good God who
loves you." That truth made all the difference.

Our fear of man feeds off of misperceptions about God. But

when we combat lies about God with the truth about him found in Scripture, we choke off this food supply. Soon our fear of others begins to shrink, while our confidence and joy in God begin to grow.

If you are a Christian, God's Word is clear: *nothing* shall separate you from the love of Christ—not tribulation, distress, persecution, famine, nakedness, danger, or sword. Do you believe that? Friend, no matter what you're facing today, in Christ, God is for you. Rejoice! The confidence that the Psalmist had can be your confidence too: "The LORD is on my side; I will not fear. What can man do to me?" (Ps. 118:6).

Reflect: God's promise to "give us all things" (Rom. 8:32) doesn't guarantee a pain-free life, nor does it mean that we always get what we want. In our limited knowledge and perspective, there are times when we don't know what's good for us—but God does. So, even when we're in the dark about the future, we can rest in the fact that God always gives good gifts to his children (see Matt. 7:11), for nothing can separate us from his love.

Act: We're often tempted to see God as stingy, and as withholding something good, in circumstances that tempt us to worry and fear. In those times, read Romans 8:32 and recall how Paul emphasizes that God did not spare his own Son for us. In response to the gracious, generous, and infinite goodness of God, repent of any wrong view of God you are aware of and commit to him afresh. Through him (this God who loves us), we are more than conquerors.

DAY 27

Learn True Contentment

Not that I am speaking of being in need, for I have learned in whatever
situation I am to be content. I know how to be brought low, and I
know how to abound. In any and every circumstance, I have learned
the secret of facing plenty and hunger, abundance and need. I can
do all things through him who strengthens me. (Phil. 4:11–13)

DISCONTENT MAKES US vulnerable to fearing others. A
man dying of thirst may be so desperate for water that he leans
over the life raft to guzzle saltwater, but this won't satisfy. Similarly, when discontent shows up in a job, relationship (or lack
thereof), circumstance, or trial, our frustration with waiting
leaves us susceptible to gulping down the saltwater of man's
praise and approval, thinking that *it* will make us happy and
whole. It's the contented person who is equipped to refuse the
easy, accessible, and unsatisfying substitutes in order to wait for
that which *can* satisfy.

Jonathan Edwards served for twenty-four years at a church in
Northampton, Massachusetts. But on June 22, 1750, he was fired.
We could expect Edwards to wallow in self-pity or bitterness.
But he didn't! One observer recorded Edwards's reaction, saying that he "received the shock, unshaken. I never saw the least
symptoms of displeasure in his countenance the whole week, but
he appeared like a man of God, whose *happiness was out of the*
reach of his enemies and whose treasure was not only a future but
a present good, overbalancing all imaginable ills of life, even to
the astonishment of many who could not be at rest without his
dismission."[1]

What *is* contentment? Look again at Philippians 4:11.
Contentment can be defined as having a sufficiency that is

independent of circumstances, conditions, or surroundings. Edwards beautifully illustrated this contentment by demonstrating *a happiness that was out of the reach of his enemies.* Can you say that of your joy?

Reflect: Contentment is easy to define but hard to sustain in our experience. How can we grow in contentment? Notice that, in verse 11, Paul says that he learned contentment. How encouraging! Even the apostle had days of discontent, but with God's help he learned contentment (just as we can). So what was his secret (see v. 12)? It was Jesus! Saying that I can do all things through Christ is not saying that by faith I can become a millionaire, ace the exam, or make the NBA. No—the context shows that "all things" meant that he could be content whether he had a feast or went hungry (see v. 12), through Christ who strengthened him. This strength was fueled by his seeing the supreme value of Christ (Phil. 3:8–9). The world may take our job, reputation, or comfort, but if our satisfaction is in Jesus, our joy is beyond the reach of our enemies.

Act: If contentment is something that we learn, then don't skip school. As he did with Paul, God often uses the school of hardship as his classroom. When you face a trial, pray that you don't grow weary under God's loving, fatherly discipline, but that you will learn and grow through it (see Heb. 12:5–6).

Act: The only way to see the surpassing value of Christ is for God to open our eyes. As you look at him in the pages of Scripture, pray with Moses, "Satisfy us in the morning with your steadfast love, that we may rejoice and be glad all our days" (Ps. 90:14).

DAY 28

Face the What-Ifs of Life

"Do not be anxious, saying, 'What shall we eat?' or 'What shall we drink?' or 'What shall we wear?' For the Gentiles seek after all these things, and your heavenly Father knows that you need them all. But seek first the kingdom of God and his righteousness, and all these things will be added to you. . . . Do not be anxious about tomorrow, for tomorrow will be anxious for itself. Sufficient for the day is its own trouble." (Matt. 6:31–34)

IF YOU'VE EVER been to the state fair, chances are that you've seen Whac-A-Mole. It's a game in which your job is to use a rubber mallet to hit toy moles that pop up at random all across the board. But before you hit one mole, another pops up; the longer you play, the harder it gets. (It's good that they give you a rubber mallet to vent your frustration!)

Sometimes life feels like a Whac-A-Mole game. We long to have a sense of control over life's problems. But as soon as we're able to whack one problem (debt, sickness, conflict, and so on), another pops up. If we fall behind, life's problems can overwhelm us and leave us anxious. We realize that we're *not* in control. We don't know when the next problem is coming, where it's coming from, and whether we have what it takes to face it.

When you look at the future, do you hear the anxious "what-ifs" whispering to your heart? *What if you don't get the job? What if they leave you? What if you let them down? What if . . . ?* To all these causes of worry in our lives, Jesus says, "Child, do not be anxious" (see Matt. 6:31). Don't be anxious?! How? Doesn't he see all the what-ifs I'm facing that I have no control over? He does. And, friend, *that's Jesus's point!* When it comes to what you need (food, drink, clothing, and so on), "Your heavenly Father knows that you need them all" (Matt. 6:32).

71

When it comes to our fight against the fear of man, God's solution is not to be our personal relations consultant whose job is to make sure that people like us. Instead, he promises to be with us. The God who is in control of all things (see Ps. 115:3), who owns all resources (see Ps. 24:1), and who loves us (see Rom. 5:8)—*that* God is with us. Knowing who God is and that he's near sets us free from living in the fear of the what-ifs to instead live in the freedom of the even-ifs. As David said in Psalm 23:4, "Even though I walk through the valley of the shadow of death, I will fear no evil, for you are with me."

Reflect: In Matthew 6, one approach Jesus takes as he addresses fear is to fix our gaze on God and his generous care (see vv. 26–30). For every glance you take at the various what-ifs of life, how often are you fixing your eyes on God as he is revealed in Scripture?

Act: It's good to plan (see Prov. 21:5), but we need to trust God with our future, not try to control it. As Jesus reminds us, each day has sufficient trouble of its own. His point is that we are to take one day at a time. You may be worried about the next five years, five months, or five days—but can you trust God for today? Can you trust him for the next five minutes? Commit your next five minutes to God, cast your burden on him, and then repeat. The Christian life isn't a matter of plugging in principles and following rules outside of a relationship; it's a moment-by-moment, day-to-day trust in God.

DAY 29

Walk in the Light

Take care, brothers, lest there be in any of you an evil, unbelieving heart, leading you to fall away from the living God. But exhort one another every day, as long as it is called "today," that none of you may be hardened by the deceitfulness of sin. (Heb. 3:12–13)

I WAS CALLED to the hospital around 1:00 a.m. On the outside, he'd seemed to be doing well. He was happily married and successful at work, had numerous friends, and was a member of our church. But no one knew what he was struggling with. He figured that he could beat sin on his own. But a few isolated instances of lust turned into flirtation, until sin began to snowball. Before long, he was maintaining multiple adulterous relationships simultaneously. That afternoon, it all came crashing down. Unable to see a way out, he tried to take his own life. What happened?

Hebrews 3:13 calls *each* of us to exhort one another. To exhort means to warn *and* encourage. Exhortation is necessary *so that none of us are hardened by the deceitfulness of sin.* Sin lies to us, whispering, "There's no harm in this! No one will find out! This will satisfy." But sin *never* delivers on its promises. No one wakes up one morning saying, "I'm going to ruin my life today!" It happens through little decisions—compromises left unchecked . . . and each time, sin hardens the heart a little more, making it easier for us to go deeper into sin. Drifting away from God is usually subtle, and apart from the grace of God, it can happen to *any* of us. That's why we are called to exhortation—the *antidote* to hardheartedness.

For years, fear had kept my friend from telling anyone about his struggle. But hitting rock bottom was a wakeup call that provided him the courage to open up. As I sat next to my friend in the

73

hospital that morning, he finally stepped into the light, confessed everything, and found relief. When folks in the church found out, they didn't shun him; they came alongside him and his family to warn *and* encourage. Ten years later, he is, by God's grace, happily married to the same woman and walking with God.

Reflect: After you've sinned, have you ever heard sin whispering, "Sure, this was wrong—but you don't need to tell anyone. Just don't do it again!" No matter how strong a resolve we have, we need the exhortation of *others* in order to overcome sin's deceitful, hardening effects. Are you willing to live in the light as God calls us to do?

Act: A doctor can't help you unless you tell her what's ailing you. In the same way, others won't know how to encourage or warn you unless you tell them the truth about your sin. As scary as it is, coming into the light with sin is necessary for us to overcome a hard heart and the fear of others that led us there in the first place. Who is one trusted friend you can confess your sin to (see Prov. 28:13; James 5:16)?

Act: The fear of man tells us to keep sin in the dark, because others would exclude us if they found out. But the thing that binds a church together isn't our performance; it's the fact that we know we are *all* sinners trusting Jesus to cleanse us (see 1 John 1:7). In that sense, a church is people who are committed to exhorting one another so that they don't drift away. Not a member of a church? One practical step is to join one that preaches the Bible.

DAY 30

Serve Your Father
Who Sees in Secret

*"Beware of practicing your righteousness before other people in order
to be seen by them, for then you will have no reward from your Father
who is in heaven. Thus, when you give to the needy, sound no trumpet
before you, as the hypocrites do in the synagogues and in the streets, that
they may be praised by others. Truly, I say to you, they have received
their reward. But when you give to the needy, do not let your left hand
know what your right hand is doing, so that your giving may be in secret.
And your Father who sees in secret will reward you." (Matt. 6:1–4)*

IT ISN'T FUN being overlooked. Whether we are snubbed for
a promotion at work or are the last one picked for a sports team,
being overlooked can make us feel worthless. One example of
this longing for significance can be seen in our social media. Like
a fisherman, we cast ideas, photos, and personal achievements
into internet waters, hoping to catch a "like" or to gain another
follower. The more followers and "likes" we have, the more
important we feel. Consequently, we look to others to validate
our significance and identity. As Os Guinness explains, "The age
of the Internet . . . is the age of the self and the selfie. The world is
full of people full of themselves. In such an age, 'I post, therefore
I am.'"[1] The problem is that looking to other people in this way
makes us a slave to their opinions.

Alternatively, Jesus offers freedom that is based on a different
approach. Instead of seeking the praise of man, we are to seek the
praise of God as our reward. Those who live *this* way have no need
of announcing what they've done, and they are free to give themselves away for the good of others, regardless of the response that

they do (or don't) get. They are so unconcerned about being seen that their right hand doesn't know what their left hand is doing (see Matt. 6:3).

This unrecognized selflessness makes no sense to a watching world. Why would anyone pay the costs of helping someone else *for nothing*? Why, if you *could* get recognition, would you do good deeds *in secret*? Because "Your Father who sees in secret will reward you" (v. 4). Christians seek a *greater* reward than the fickle praise of man. Knowing that God is in secret, we know that he sees what is done in secret. The world may overlook us, others can't see our hearts, and our sacrifice may go without thanks—but God sees and promises a reward. This truth frees us from enslavement to the opinions of others so that we can give of ourselves with joy.

Reflect: We may not be so bold so as to *blatantly* promote ourselves, but we can do it in more subtle ways. For example, false humility ("Oh, I'm no good") can be a quiet way for us to fish for compliments ("No! You're amazing!"). What are ways in which you're tempted to exalt yourself in the eyes of others?

Act: One way that we demonstrate our trust in Jesus's promise of a *future* reward is by associating with the lowly (see Rom. 12:16)—with people who don't boost our image but are nonetheless precious because they're created in God's image. As an act of such faith, who is someone you can love and serve whom others may overlook? What act of generosity, service, or virtue can you do in secret, believing that God sees and will reward you?

DAY 31

Pray for a United Heart

Teach me your way, O LORD, that I may walk in your truth; unite my heart to fear your name. (Ps. 86:11)

WHAT DOES A *divided* heart look like? As a child I remember more than once going to Mom with a request: "Mom, can I have dessert? Can I stay up later? Can I get the toy?" If I got the answer that I *wanted*, my mission was complete. But if she gave me an answer that I *didn't* like, the answer that I *feared* she would give, what was I to do? Go to Dad, of course! If I could get the desired response before Mom and Dad discussed it, I would get what I wanted without breaking the rules.

In the same way, a divided heart comes to God ready to obey as long as we like what he says. A divided heart has the *appearance* of godliness, because we *are* coming to him asking for wisdom, provision, and guidance! But it is more unstable than it is godly (see James 1:8). A divided heart has competing allegiances and looks for the easiest path it can take, while maintaining the image of obedience.

In Psalm 86:11, David asks God, "Unite my heart to fear your name." Why would he need to ask that? Because his heart was divided! Like David, our hearts come in parts. If we could hit the pause button during our day and look at our heart, we might find one part threatened by what's happening at work, another part fearful about getting sick, another part threatened by what we heard on the news, another part fearful about the kids, or another part threatened by money.

I assume that you, like me, *want* to fear God with a united heart. So how do we get there? Similarly to David, we recognize that a united heart is a *gift* from God. As the hymn reminds us, we ask God for his help: "Come, thou fount of ev'ry blessing, tune my heart to sing thy grace; streams of mercy, never ceasing, call for songs of loudest praise. Teach me some melodious sonnet, sung by flaming tongues above."[1] Our hearts tend to conform to the world and to fear that which the world fears. For that reason, they're like an instrument that needs tuning from time to time. As God, the great heart-tuner, unites our hearts to fear his name, we will find ourselves once again singing that *melodious sonnet, sung by flaming tongues above.*

Reflect: Take an inventory of your heart. Can you hear where it's out of tune? Can you identify where it's fearing or feeling threatened by something *other* than God?

Act: Thankfully, God doesn't require us to "get it together" before we come to him. Through Christ, we can approach him confidently and pour out our hearts to him (see Ps. 62:8). Take a moment to bring God all the parts of your divided heart— the concerns, anxieties, and fears—so that he can tune your heart to sing his praise.

God, I bring you my divided heart and pray that you would unite it to fear your name. Help me not to fear man. Help me to accept your will, no matter what it is, and to trust that it is good, because you are completely good. Help me to rejoice and to rest in you. In Jesus's name, amen!

Conclusion

ON A LONG road trip, the question our boys ask over and over is (you guessed it) "Are we there yet?" It's hard being patient—especially when you don't have a sense of how long your journey will be. But patience isn't just a challenge for kids on a road trip. Whether it was the Israelites grumbling in the wilderness (see Num. 11), the psalmist asking, "How long" (Ps. 13:1), or the disciples wanting to know God's timetable (see Acts 1:6–7), the people of God have found waiting to be difficult since the beginning.

This is helpful to remember because, in the fight against sin, it's easy for us to be impatient. We might ask, in our frustration, "Why am I not further along than I am? Why am I *still* battling with my fear of others? Why hasn't God taken it away once and for all?" As Christians, we are painfully inconsistent at times. We long for the fight for faith to be over, to see God face-to-face, and to walk not by faith but by sight. John Newton, the author of "Amazing Grace" and a former slave trader turned Christian, made this point well. Near the end of his life, he looked back to write,

> I am not what I ought to be—ah, how imperfect and deficient! I am not what I wish to be—I abhor what is evil, and I would cleave to what is good! I am not what I hope to be—soon, soon shall I put off mortality, and with mortality all sin and imperfection. Yet, though I am not what I ought to be, nor what I wish to be, nor what I hope to be, I can truly say, I am not what I once was; a slave to sin and Satan; and I can heartily join with the apostle, and acknowledge, "By the grace of God I am what I am."[1]

On this side of heaven, we live in what theologians call the "already/not-yet" period of the kingdom of God. Jesus's arrival ushered in the kingdom of God (see Matt. 12:28; Mark 1:15). Consequently, God's people experience growth in the grace and knowledge of God. We fear man less than we did before—we are not as controlled by others' opinions and we enjoy more of the freedom that comes from fearing God. We know the blessing of God's rule in our life! Yet sin remains. One day there will be *no* more tears, sorrow, sin, or death (see Rev. 21:1–4). One day there will be *no* fear of man. But, until we die or Christ returns, we must *fight* for faith and put sin to death.

I wish I could tell you I'm completely free from the fear of man in my own life, but I'm not. Like John Newton, I confess that I am not what I ought to be, nor what I wish to be, nor what I hope to be. And yet I am not what I once was. By the grace of God, I am what I am! I am still in the fight—and, I suspect, so are you. That fight can become wearisome. We, like the saints of old (or like kids on a long trip), can become impatient, grumble, and complain. That's why we cannot win this fight or finish the race alone. We need the help of God's Spirit, the encouragement of his Word, and the support of a local church. So rely on the Spirit, devour God's Word, and lean on the brothers and sisters you have in your local church. As the apostle Paul encourages us, "Let us not grow weary of doing good, for in due season we will reap, if we do not give up" (Gal. 6:9).

Battling our fear of others is hard, but it's worth it! Why? Because our fight against this fear is a fight to know and trust God, and he is our greatest reward. "Oh, how abundant is your goodness, which you have stored up for those who fear you" (Ps. 31:19).

Acknowledgments

The fear of the LORD is the beginning of wisdom, and the knowledge of the Holy One is insight. (Prov. 9:10)

KATIE AND I celebrated twelve years of marriage this year, and for her I am profoundly thankful. Over the years she has modeled how to trust confidently in God, how to show generosity, and how to fight for faith when circumstances strain our trust in God. Learning to lead as a husband and father with her as my wife has been a joy. On more than one occasion, I've been tempted to balk at the "risks" that come with making a godly decision. Having a wife who fears the Lord has been God's gift to put steel into my spine in those moments. Proverbs 31:30 says, "A woman who fears the LORD is to be praised." Katie, you are an excellent wife— far more precious than jewels!

I am thankful to Deepak Reju, who has been a dear friend over the years. This project has been a good excuse for us to work together, and I am thankful for your wise suggestions, edits, encouragement, and prayers. What a joy to partner together in gospel work. Thank you for your leadership and help!

To the elders at First Baptist Church of Upper Marlboro (Tony, Danny, Bill, Rob, Mike, and Tyrone), thank you for your support and encouragement on this project as well. I thank God for the wisdom he has given you all, for the shepherding care and concern you have for our church family, and for the ways that you love and support me and my family.

To our church family, I thank God for the ways that you love him, love each other, and hunger for his Word. It is a joy to call First Baptist Church our home—to labor alongside you as we seek to grow in the fear of God and the knowledge of the Holy One.

Notes

Tips for Reading This Devotional

1. See Jonathan Leeman, *Reverberation: How God's Word Brings Light, Freedom, and Action to His People* (Chicago: Moody, 2011), 19.

Introduction

1. Edward T. Welch, *When People Are Big and God Is Small: Overcoming Peer Pressure, Codependency, and the Fear of Man* (Phillipsburg, NJ: P&R Publishing, 1997), 14.

Day 3: Watch Out! It's a Trap!

1. See Bruce K. Waltke, *The Book of Proverbs: Chapters 15–31*, The New International Commentary on the Old Testament (Grand Rapids: Eerdmans, 2005), 452.

Day 6: The Fear of Falling

1. Tim Keller, *Counterfeit Gods: The Empty Promises of Money, Sex, and Power, and the Only Hope That Matters* (2009; repr., New York: Penguin, 2016), 109; quoting from Diana R. Henriques, "Madoff, Apologizing, Is Given 150 Years," *New York Times*, June 30, 2009; and "Bernard Madoff Gets 150 Years in Jail for Epic Fraud," *Bloomberg*, available from *Business Standard*, January 19, 2013, https://www.business-standard.com/article/economy-policy/bernard-madoff-gets-150-years-in-jail-for-epic-fraud-109063000045_1.html.

Day 7: The Surprising Source of Confidence

1. Oswald Chambers, "Psalm 128: Seemliness of Sanctity," in *The Pilgrim's Song Book* (repr., London: Simpkin Marshall, 1941).

Day 8: Confidence in Your Insufficiency

1. See John Piper, "Dana, Doug and an APTAT Recap," Desiring God, accessed November 27, 2018, http://www.desiringgod.org /articles/dana-doug-and-an-aptat-recap.

Day 9: The Grasshopper Syndrome

1. Oswald Chambers, "Man's Weakness—God's Strength," *Missionary Crusader*, December 1964, 7.

Day 11: Don't Take It Personally

1. See entry "1016: כָּעַס (kă ʿăs)," *Theological Wordbook of the Old Testament*, ed. R. Laird Harris, Gleason L. Archer Jr., and Bruce K. Waltke (Chicago: Moody Press, 1980), 451.

Day 12: You Shall Not Covet

1. See H. D. McDonald, "Envy," in *New Bible Dictionary*, ed. D. R. W. Wood et al., 3rd ed. (Downers Grove, IL: InterVarsity Press, 1996), 325.

Day 13: Overcome Your Fear of Others by Fearing God

1. Timothy Keller, *The Meaning of Marriage: Facing the Complexities of Marriage with the Wisdom of God* (New York: Penguin, 2013), 44.

Day 14: Fan the Flame

1. Roland H. Bainton, *Here I Stand: A Life of Martin Luther* (repr., Nashville: Abingdon Press, 1978), 181–82.
2. Michael Reeves, *The Unquenchable Flame: Discovering the Heart of the Reformation* (Nashville: B&H Academic, 2010), 56.

Day 19: Know God's Purpose for Your Life

1. Augustine, *Confessions: A New Translation by Sarah Ruden* (New York: Modern Library, 2017), 3.
2. Emily Dickinson, "Fame Is a Fickle Food," in *The Single Hound: Poems of a Lifetime* (Boston: Little, Brown, and Company, 1915), 6.
3. Westminster Shorter Catechism, answer 1.

Day 20: Embrace the Accusations
1. Alfred J. Poirier, "The Cross and Criticism," *The Journal of Biblical Counseling* 17, no. 3 (Spring 1999): 17. (The ideas from Poirer's article were very helpful.)

Day 21: Fight Fear with Prayer
1. H. B. Charles Jr., *It Happens after Prayer: Biblical Motivation for Believing Prayer* (Chicago: Moody, 2013), 16.

Day 22: Look to Your Future Hope
1. See James R. Edwards, *The Gospel According to Mark*, The Pillar New Testament Commentary (Grand Rapids: Eerdmans, 2002), 449.

Day 23: Compete to Love, Not to Be Loved
1. C. S. Lewis, *Mere Christianity* (New York: Macmillan, 1952; repr., New York: Harper Collins, 2001), 122.

Day 25: Fight Fear with Thankfulness
1. See Paul David Tripp, "Fearless Forever" (lecture, CCEF National Conference, Valley Forge, PA, November 3, 2007).

Day 27: Learn True Contentment
1. David Hall, diary entry, Massachusetts Historical Society, Boston; quoted in Iain H. Murray, *Jonathan Edwards: A New Biography* (Carlisle, PA: Banner of Truth, 1987), 327, emphasis added.

Day 30: Serve Your Father Who Sees in Secret
1. Os Guinness, *Fool's Talk: Recovering the Art of Christian Persuasion* (Downers Grove, IL: InterVarsity Press, 2015), 15.

Day 31: Pray for a United Heart
1. Robert Robinson, "Come Thou Fount of Every Blessing," 1758.

Conclusion
1. Quoted in D. A. Carson, *The God Who Is There: Finding Your Place in God's Story* (Grand Rapids: Baker Books, 2010), 196.

Suggested Resources for the Fight

Burroughs, Jeremiah. *The Rare Jewel of Christian Contentment.* 1648. Reprint, Carlisle, PA: Banner of Truth Trust, 2000. [This classic has withstood the test of time and proven to be a great help to many Christians. Discontent is a close cousin to the fear of man. Burroughs is faithful to show how the gospel quiets the restless and discontent heart. Instead of looking to the world to supply our greatest needs, he points us to the One who truly satisfies.]

Saer, Orlando. *Big God: How to Approach Suffering, Spread the Gospel, Make Decisions and Pray in the Light of a God Who Really Is in the Driving Seat of the World.* Tain, UK: Christian Focus, 2014. [Knowing that we fear man because God has become small in our hearts and minds, Saer provides a wonderful meditation on the greatness of God. This book provides a sample of the countless applications that come from seeing God rightly.]

Spurgeon, Charles. "Fear Not." Sermon, London, October 4, 1857. Available online at https://www.spurgeongems.org/vols1-3/chs 156.pdf. [In this sermon, Charles Spurgeon expounds on Isaiah 41:14 to help us recognize our own weakness and the wonderful provision of strength that God promises his children.]

Welch, Edward T. *When People Are Big and God Is Small: Overcoming Peer Pressure, Codependency, and the Fear of Man.* Phillipsburg, NJ: P&R, 1997. [If you'd like to do more thinking on what the Bible says about the fear of man, Ed Welch's book is a must-read. The book is packed with Scripture, pastoral in nature, and extremely insightful. Welch helps the reader see how fearing others affects us, in ways we may have been unaware of, and points us to the greatness of God as a remedy.]

**BIBLICAL
COUNSELING
COALITION**

The Biblical Counseling Coalition (BCC) is passionate about enhancing and advancing biblical counseling globally. We accomplish this through broadcasting, connecting, and collaborating.

Broadcasting promotes gospel-centered biblical counseling ministries and resources to bring hope and healing to hurting people around the world. We promote biblical counseling in a number of ways: through our *15:14* podcast, website (biblicalcounselingcoalition.org), partner ministry, conference attendance, and personal relationships.

Connecting biblical counselors and biblical counseling ministries is a central component of the BCC. The BCC was founded by leaders in the biblical counseling movement who saw the need for and the power behind building a strong global network of biblical counselors. We introduce individuals and ministries to one another to establish gospel-centered relationships.

Collaboration is the natural outgrowth of our connecting efforts. We truly believe that biblical counselors and ministries can accomplish more by working together. The BCC Confessional Statement, which is a clear and comprehensive definition of biblical counseling, was created through the cooperative effort of over thirty leading biblical counselors. The BCC has also published a three-part series of multi-contributor works that bring theological wisdom and practical expertise to pastors, church leaders, counseling practitioners, and students. Each year we are able to facilitate the production of numerous resources, including books, articles, videos, audio resources, and a host of other helps for biblical counselors. Working together allows us to provide robust resources and develop best practices in biblical counseling so that we can hone the ministry of soul care in the church.

To learn more about the BCC, visit biblicalcounselingcoalition.org.

More on the Fear of Others

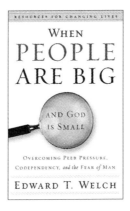

"Need people less. Love people more. That's the author's challenge. . . . He's talking about a tendency to hold other people in awe, to be controlled and mastered by them, to depend on them for what God alone can give. . . . [Welch] proposes an antidote: the fear of God . . . the believer's response to God's power, majesty and not least his mercy."
— *Dallas Morning News*

"Refreshingly biblical . . . brimming with helpful, readable, practical insight."
— **John MacArthur**, president of The Master's College and Seminary

"Ed Welch is a good physician of the soul. This book is enlightening, convicting, and encouraging. I highly recommend it."
— **Jerry Bridges**, author of Trusting God

More on the Fear of Others

"From his years of counseling experience, Lou Priolo has developed a work that exposes many of the prideful manifestations of people-pleasing, while also walking the reader through the biblical process of repentance from the heart. This is a book that God can use greatly to change lives."

    —**Stuart Scott**, associate professor of biblical counseling, the Southern Baptist Theological Seminary

"Even if you think you do not have this weakness, you may be convicted that you do! The strengths of this book are the biblical principles, its charts with wrong compared to right ways of thinking, and its counsel on how to become a 'God pleaser.' I am very pleased to have this resource for helping people."

    —**Martha Peace**, author of *The Excellent Wife* and *Damsels in Distress*

Was this book helpful to you?
Consider writing a review online.
The author appreciates your feedback!

Or write to P&R at editorial@prpbooks.com
with your comments. We'd love to hear from you.